A
SHORT WALK
WITH
EMMA

BRIAN H. RHEN

FOUNDER

Cover design by Todd Simpson

Founder Nonfiction by *Businessing Magazine*

First Edition

ISBN: 978-1-7378262-0-0

Some names and identifying details have been changed to protect the privacy of individuals.

To my beloved wife, Missy

lover of God, my best friend, an amazing mom,
so wise, a beauty, and
His grace to me.

CONTENTS

AUTHOR'S NOTE

S IMPLY PUT, DEATH BRINGS PERSPECTIVE to life. Although I wrote eighty percent of this book back in the summer of 2002 as a way out of my deep sadness (and thank goodness I did because I would've never remembered all the details fifteen years later), my perspective on Emma's death and our grief had become even more refined by the time I began typing again in 2017. I was amazed by the way the scenes from May 1999 to September 2001 came alive again, not to mention how the core truths of the lessons learned remained consistent.

Looking back, I realize that my inability to complete the initial writing was a combination of life circumstances and my need to mature. Over time, my soul deepened with God, my motives for writing purified, my fear lessened, my sweet mom, Sally, died in December 2017, my kids grew into their teens and twenties, my dad, Bob, encountered Parkinson's disease, my years of sitting with grieving folks multiplied, my joy of putting words to paper increased, and my timing became more urgent as I entered life in my fifties.

Fredrick Buechner stated, "The place God calls you is the place where your deep gladness and the world's deep hunger meet."[1] Hence, as I have typed my way through this project, I am assured of the first part of his statement being true. Yet, I humbly hope the second part becomes reality for you, the reader, as you journey through the lessons.

This project has brought me joy in so many unexpected ways. First, in the amount of tears shed. As I have typed with music streaming into my ears and down into my soul, it tapped an endless well of emotion burrowed inside me over and over again. Each time I typed, I looked forward to this unknown-but-needed release. Though some of the tears were for the loss of my precious little one, Emma, I found that most of my tears flowed from the gratitude I had for the engagement with the people in our story. At other times, the well bubbled over because of the immense appreciation I had for how God guided us through, gave us a way out, blessed us with more, and used it all for such good in time.

More and more, I have come to realize that some of the greatest gifts given to me have included Emma's death, the addiction in my family of origin, plus most of my other disappointments and failures. These unique gifts have taught me the most significant lessons in life. Plus, they have enabled me to connect with others in a manner that could not have happened without these experiences. I have heard it said that pain is our greatest teacher. Though so true, upon reflection, I wish for myself and others that our ability to learn would increase in times of comfort rather than when facing such enormous discomfort.

endless thanks

When your first writing endeavor takes you almost twenty years to complete, you realize it is not possible without the support of many others. I have such overwhelming appreciation for the following folks:

My wife, Missy—for sharing your faith with me, which changed everything.

My kids—for listening to me talk about it for years.

My oldest, Sadie—for always encouraging me to finish this book.

My Rhen, Morrill, Hirsh, Henry, and Junker clans—for providing a caring family base that stabilized us through it all.

My friends close and far—for all the encouraging notes and calls that reminded us that we were not alone.

My former Latrobe High School basketball coach Ray Zsolcsak, and players, Jim Biss, Neal and Keith Fenton—for hosting the Emma Rhen Memorial Golf Outing in 2003.

My favorite doctor, Emma's cardiologist, Dr. Jeff Feinstein, and many of the staff at Lucile Packard Children's Hospital—for showing us compassion, professionalism, and true friendship.

My editor, Jessica Dawson—for being a gift given by God who re-sparked my passion for this project and gently edited, while reminding me of three things that kept me going:

"Don't let your perfectionism be the enemy of your creativity."

"Write fast enough to outrun self -doubt."

"You cannot edit a blank page."

My editing friends, Lisa Chan, Kirsetin Morello, Patty Naff, Julie Steele and Daisy Segal—for using your expertise to refine the telling of this story.

My (deceased) buddy, Steve Bryan—for having such a big heart for Emma and for teaching me to feel.

My loyal friend, Jeff Smith—for believing in my potential from the start and being present at the perfect time.

My long-time colleague and dear brother, Gary Gaddini—for sharing so many seasons of grief and joy.

My best man, Anthony Mejia—for standing by me and always being willing to have an Emma conversation.

And finally, my many other colleagues and friends at Peninsula Covenant Church—for carrying us in prayer during the journey, allowing me to grow up as I have served pastorally for over twenty-five years, and for making the Emma Rhen Memorial Park a reality.

Beyond the lessons declared in this clarifying journey, what I have learned the most along the way is that we are all grieving something, yet God is for and with us.

To Him be the glory because of His great love and faithfulness.

Contrary to what might be expected, I look back on experiences that at the time seemed especially desolating and painful, with particular satisfaction.

Indeed, I can say with complete truthfulness that everything I have learned in my seventy-five years in this world, everything that has truly enhanced and enlightened my existence, has been through affliction and not through happiness, whether pursued or attained.

This of course is what the Cross signifies.

Malcolm Muggeridge

INTRODUCTION

CALLED OUT TO MY DAUGHTER, "Sadie, please stop at that pole ahead, we need to wait for Emma. Emma! Emma! Come on you silly girl. Catch up to us!" With her bottom lip leading, Emma stood two house lengths back on the sidewalk, smirking, standing still, rolling her wide blue eyes, with her hands at her side and gently said, "Hold me." As usual, I headed on back to get her. When I bent down to pick her up, I could hear her panting and feel her heart racing as she locked her legs and arms around my side. I thought to myself, "Just another short walk with Emma." Then, we raced off together to catch her big sister. Sadie, seventeen months older and almost four, waited patiently at the telephone pole pushing the oversized nail that had been driven into it. She was pretending it was the crosswalk button. As we jogged to catch up, Emma patted my head gently and playfully said, "Dada. Dada."

As her walks were short, so was Emma's life. A brief season was all we were blessed with—two years and just shy of four months. She was born May 12, 1999 with a congenital heart defect, Hypoplastic Left Heart Syndrome (underdeveloped left ventricle). Without medical intervention, she would not have survived even a few weeks. Doctors discovered it when we rushed her to the emergency room only a week after her birth because she was having trouble breathing and eating. After stabilizing her, we were given the options of a heart transplant, three reconstructive heart surgeries, or doing nothing at all for her condition. We chose the three surgeries.

Emma had her first heart surgery at two weeks old. It went well and she recovered speedily. At four months old, she had her second operation and was released from the hospital after eight days. Two years later on September 5, 2001, Emma had a successful third surgery, however she was unable to overcome complications of an infection during the recovery. On the morning of September 8, 2001, we released her from a respirator.

Though her life was brief, it was long enough for an enormous Emma space to be carved into our lives, leaving a deep emptiness within us. In the foreword of C.S. Lewis' *A Grief Observed*, his stepson writes of Lewis' pain regarding the loss of his wife of a just a few years:

"It almost seems cruel that her death was delayed long enough for him to grow to love her so completely that she filled his world as the greatest gift that God had given him, and she died and left him alone in a place that her presence in his life had created for him."[2]

So too was our short walk with Emma, so dramatic in circumstance, so rich in emotion, that it seemed to bond and age my wife and me in years beyond comprehension, while leaving us yearning for more and more in her absence.

I believe Emma's life was intended by God the Father, our divine Creator, to be short, for it was the only thing that could get our full attention. Our experience has shown us and others that we needed the drama of Emma's life to help us become more like the individuals God intended for us to be.

I realize that last statement seems crazy. Am I possibly conveying the notion that a loving God allows circumstances, even the death of another, to change us? Or that He actually has an intentional purpose and character development plan for each one of us that we might be missing?

My hope is that as you read on, you will face the tension of these issues and grasp your own learnings. From a personal standpoint, our short walk with Emma has reoriented our lives to the degree that our life focus, daily priorities, marriage, friendships, and understanding of God have all been radically enhanced. And, while the pain of death and the void of loss seem to have no true earthly replacement, these lessons from God have acted as salve for our wounds— providing peace and perspective amidst the pain.

Each chapter in this book includes a window into the brief journey with Emma from the first week of her life up to and beyond her dying day, along with corresponding lessons learned and a few reflection questions to help you, individually or as a group, integrate the lessons into your own life.

My desire is that your perspective on life, God, relationships, suffering, and death would be transformed by what God gave us through Emma.

What we believe about God is the most
important thing about us.

Our belief or lack of it inevitably translates itself into our
actions, our attitudes, and our view of the world.

A.W. Tozer

LESSON ONE

life is about something greater than ourselves

I SAT AT MY KITCHEN TABLE JUST BEFORE MIDNIGHT on May 22, 1999 and opened my Bible. As usual, I was behind in my scheduled reading. Along my brief journey as a follower of Christ, the Bible, along with the mysterious power of the Holy Spirit, had been essential in shaping my character, actions, and life perspective to become more as God intended. As I turned the pages of my Bible during that sitting, I was not attempting to refine my character or find forgiveness for another round of selfish actions. This time, I was searching for perspective.

Two days earlier, our daughter, Emma Grace Rhen, had been diagnosed with Hypoplastic Left Heart Syndrome. This meant she had an underdeveloped left ventricle, causing the heart to be unable to maintain proper functioning without immediate medical intervention. The traumatic events of the week and a house filled with family and friends late into the night had disengaged me from my attempts at an early morning devotional ritual. Even in the midst of the chaos, I was determined to get back on track with my devotional reading, which had left off in the book of Job.

My determination was also sparked by my desire to finish *The Daily Walk Bible* that was designed to help me read through the entire Bible in a year's time, something I had never done. Although the mere goal of it had been enough to keep me motivated, I was often astonished by the manner each daily reading brought insight or related specifically to my life. This happened even in the midst of the most uninspiring sections, like the book of Leviticus (filled with Jewish laws). I often said that this proved that God's Word was alive and active.

There, in the midnight hour, I prayed and opened up my Bible where I had left off, the one marked May 18. I had no idea that this act of prideful obedience would turn into a spiritual journey that was well beyond the earthly goal I set for myself.

Although the hour was late and I was worn out from the past few days' events, the biblical passages and notes for the reader caught my attention and snapped me into alertness. The passages for May 18 found me in Job chapters 8-10, and I began to intensely relate to the words of Job, a man of great faith, but who was experiencing extreme suffering (the loss of his family, wealth, and health) and questioning God.

> "Your hands shaped me and made me. Will you now turn
> and destroy me? Remember that you molded me like clay.
> Will you now turn me to dust again? Did you not pour me
> out like milk and curdle me like cheese, clothe me with skin

and flesh and knit me together with bones and sinews? You gave me life and showed me kindness, and in your providence watched over my spirit."

Job 10:8-12

The reader's notes summarized this passage with a simple line that read, "The best of saints have borne the worst of sufferings."[3]

I pondered, "Could this be related to our situation with Emma?" A saint in this context was viewed as one who had set themselves apart for God. Though I was learning what it meant to be a saint, I was much more familiar with being a sinner. As a sinner, I had experienced the painful consequences of my sinfulness, but as a supposed saint, I had not yet really experienced the worst of suffering.

As I continued on to the readings for May 19, Job's words sank into my heart and stung as he spoke of the lifespan of man and the finality of death:

"A person's days are determined; you have decreed the number of his months and have set limits he cannot exceed… But a man dies and is laid low; he breathes his last and is no more. As the water of a lake dries up or a riverbed becomes parched and dry, so he lies down and does not rise; till the heavens are no more, people will not awake or be roused from their sleep."

Job 14:5, 10-12

Then a rush of fear ignited within me and a flood of tears rolled down my face as I pondered the reader's note that summarized the passages for May 20. I read the line: "Your ability to learn depends in part on your ability to relinquish what you have."[4]

I read that line over and over again, and in a panic, I wrote with my red pencil above the line, *"Emma?"* I went back to the passage on the previous page and wrote a little larger in red pencil, *"Will Emma Die?"* I sat, sobbing, my mind racing, trying to determine if I had just heard directly from God or if I was delirious from sleep deprivation and over-connecting the spiritual dots.

With a mixture of intrigue and fear, I kept reading. Looking back, I am shocked that I had the nerve to write, "Teach Me!" in the same margin where I had written "Emma?" By the end of my midnight devotional time, I felt most like Job in Chapter 17 when he says, "My spirit is broken." But I could find solace in the May 21 summary which stated, "When Job's world came crashing down around him, he no doubt, faced an avalanche of emotional responses: fear, frustration, anger, bitterness, confusion, bewilderment. Unknown to Job, a celestial drama was unfolding between God and Satan—with Job as the center of attention."[5]

As it turned out, those passages of Scripture and the reader's notes were a foreshadowing of the drama that was to unfold over the next two years and four months of our life. In retrospect, my wife and I believe we were spared by God's grace from losing our daughter early in this process, for we needed time to learn that life was about something greater than ourselves.

Though I had developed a personal relationship with God through Jesus Christ and had been attempting to live a life that was seeking His will more than my own over the previous eight years, I was still very much consumed with my agenda, meaning all that I hoped and dreamed would happen in my small world during my lifetime. Little did I know that with Emma's birth and the devastating diagnosis of her heart condition, my selfish perspective on life was about to completely transform.

the tension

On May 12, 1999, Emma had been born seemingly healthy, but around 3:30 a.m. on May 20, my wife, Missy, awakened me over her concern that Emma would not breastfeed and was having trouble breathing. After reluctantly taking my not-so-wise advice to wait until morning to go to the hospital, she sent me out in the wee hours of the morning for a breast pump we'd left at a friend's house. In the meantime, the wise on-call nurse asked Missy to put Emma up to the phone so she could listen to her breathe. Upon hearing Emma struggle, the nurse instructed Missy to get Emma to the hospital as soon as possible. When I returned from retrieving the breast pump and caught the end of the conversation, I knew we were headed to the emergency room at Stanford Hospital in Palo Alto, California.

After a turbulent time in the emergency room, Emma was stabilized, and an agonizing wait followed as tests were run. Three doctors delivered her diagnosis and explained three options to us. It was by God's grace, via the wisdom of my wife and that incredible on-call nurse that we even had the opportunity to consider options.

The options were: a heart transplant, a three-stage reconstructive surgery, or doing nothing at all. Nurses in the neonatal intensive care unit (NICU) informed us that parents in fifty percent of similar cases chose to do nothing, which always resulted in death within ten days. Our doctors stated that a complete heart transplant would be complicated because of the potentially long wait for an organ, the risk of rejection, and the potential for developmental side effects from anti-rejection drugs. Logic, along with the doctors' bias against a transplant, leaned us toward the third option of a three-stage reconstructive surgery.

We were told that Emma would have a seventy percent chance of making it through the entire process. Three surgeries during her first three years of life would convert her three-chamber heart into a more efficient two-chamber heart. The first surgery would need to take place within the next six days if we chose this option, but there were no guarantees. Plus, there still would be a possible need for a heart transplant in her late teens.

At this point, my internal tension was at its highest level. Besides barely grasping all the unfamiliar medical jargon, this unfolding drama was a major interruption in my life regardless of which option we chose. I had just become a participant in something of which I had wanted no part. My calendar was filled to the max and timelines for important things were in process. Although I had been married almost seven years, had an older child, and thought I had already learned a lot about being selfless, I found myself falling back into a default mode which was simply—life is about ME!

the default mode

Looking back, I realize that unfamiliarity breeds anxiety and fear. In that state, we have the likely potential to fall back into what I call our default mode. The default mode is similar to the Times New Roman font of a word processing program that has no desire or courage to attempt to be something else. The default mode is our comfort zone that holds us back from breaking through into new territory, attitudes, or skills.

If you listen closely enough to yourself or anyone else, you can hear the default mode. It complains, makes excuses, accuses, lies, looks out for number one, criticizes others and everything, while living in fear instead of in faith and hope. Theologically, the default mode is the sinful, prideful, selfish side of us that wants nothing to do with the self-reflection, accountability, and blessings that come with living into the likeness of God. This mode ignores and denies that the loving Father has sent a resurrected Son, a powerful Spirit, and the promise of an abundant life that comes with challenges. The default mode lives for self and not out of gratitude for understanding that God is willingly with us throughout the journey.

Since I was so entrenched in my self-absorbed default mode, my ability to make a decision based on what God wanted in our circumstance seemed impossible. Practically, from a non-spiritual standpoint, choosing between the three options seemed like a no-brainer. I thought to myself, "I am at one of the best pediatric heart facilities in the world. These people are the experts. Just listen to them." But, personally, from my selfish perspective, all I could think about was how this decision was going to wreak havoc on my life. However, the best thought I had was regarding my wife's character and spirituality. I knew her well enough to know that she was less likely to be trapped in my selfish thought spiral. That is one of the main reasons I married her and felt so blessed, time and again, that God had placed her in my life.

Over the next twenty-four hours, the clock ticked closer to the time when we had to give our answer to the doctors. My mind raced with questions and thoughts that were stuck in default mode.

Was I going to have a disabled child or a medically impaired one even if we choose the transplant or three surgeries? Three surgeries would interrupt our life, my schedule—medicines, doctor visits, prescriptions getting filled, possible experimental medical procedure options, getting educated about the process—and who was going to pay for all this? And what was this going to cost us emotionally in our home and marriage?

I considered my wife's wise words that she often stated, "If you are going to add something new into your life, it makes sense that something else is going to have to go or suffer." This raised my anxiety level and made me think, "What am I really going to have to give up?"

My thoughts about our hope of moving away from California and heading back east so we could buy a home and really settle down, which had repeatedly been hindered by various life events, immediately came to mind. Would this lock us into medical care in the Bay Area, since Lucile Packard Children's Hospital at Stanford had the best outcomes? So, would we NEVER leave this overpriced state?

Moreover, I was also in my last month of seminary, getting my master's degree after four-and-a-half long, brutal years, and I yearned to go two more so I could get a dual degree in counseling. How was I going to finish the huge papers I had not even started, even if I decided to get out now with one degree and graduate in six weeks? And I was about to kick off a new evening gathering at our church, which I was leading—people were counting on me; this was my big opportunity, and I had a huge team meeting that upcoming Sunday. And what about our marriage? And what would be the impact of all the attention shifting from our first child, Sadie, onto this new special-needs child? To make it all worse, the endless recurring thought that popped up between all the others: How could I be so selfish? Question upon question, mixed with layers of guilt and shame. My default mode was smothering me.

the tension mounts

As my default mode raged on, I found I was unable to focus on the bigger picture of the potential lesson(s) God was attempting to teach because my perspective had become so small—it was all about me. I believe this is common for most in the midst of crisis. Psychologically, this is called getting flooded or survival mode. Spiritually, many refer to it as desolation or moving away from God instead of towards Him. Hence, I found my irrational thoughts pulling me to the extreme opposite of faith, which for me, is always fear. These thoughts were built upon my desire for convenience, physical comfort, and emotional control.

I bottomed out with the thought, "Would it not be easier to let her go? Others have done it." Looking at Emma, almost unidentifiable, strapped to a miniature bed under a heat lamp with only a diaper on and tubes coming out from all over, I rationalized more and more. My mind flashed to the struggle in the emergency room when no one, I mean no one, was able to find a blood vessel to put in an IV, until the tenth try. The marks on her body were still visible and the visions of panic amongst a veteran trauma unit team were fresh.

Her quality of life was at a low and the future was unknown. No way could she ever live like her older sister was living. I was wrestling with the thought that one out of two families did nothing in similar situations. The hospital staff told me that some stayed and others went home to have a more quiet and peaceful releasing process of their child over the course of a few days. "Why not?" I thought. We could have more kids. Emma would not have to suffer, and the issues complicating our life would all go away. Seminary could be finished, our marriage could be protected, our first daughter could receive the proper attention, and a new evening gathering at our church could be launched. And come on! I was not that attached anyway. She wasn't even weeks old—just ten days!

Oh, how hopeless and limited are the avenues of the mind when driven by culture, fear, and a lack of faith! The default mode can be so powerfully deceptive.

As a couple, when we brought up the third option of doing nothing, it was quickly treated like a non-option. But knowing Missy's decision-making process, I concluded she would have had to at least consider the option of doing nothing. Her rational mind had to think of it. However, I also conceded that her natural loving, nurturing, motherly instinct would detour her from the avenue of that selfish thought. Realizing that her instincts had most likely saved Emma the night she crashed at home, I was once again thankful for how she balanced me in our marriage.

My tension culminated at home in the shower. There, with the water streaming full force, I sobbed in ways I never had before. It was like there was a longing in my soul that needed to be released. As I pounded the tile, I finally said to God out loud as I tried to catch my breath between gasps, "Please Lord, take this situation away from us." Many times prior to that moment, I had wanted Him to let her go so we did not have to come to terms with this decision. In those moments, I felt overwhelming guilt and shame. Where was my faith?

How much I yearned for the more comfortable way out when confronted with such unfamiliarity, fear, and complexity. Oh, how the humanity of my soul could be so misguided by my emotions! But I knew God could handle my dismay. The complaints in the Psalms and the words of Jesus were my proof. And for that I was utterly grateful to Him. Where else and to whom could I declare such a thing about my sweet daughter, His creation? I needed to get it out and come to terms with the fact that life was about something greater than myself.

lesson confirmed from above

Fortunately, in my eight prior years of attempting to walk with God, there had been some other experiences that could help counterbalance my default mode of selfishness. The first was when Missy and I were praying during her first pregnancy with Sadie. I was convicted that the only reason I was praying for a healthy child was because I could not handle the challenges of a disabled or deformed child. However, halfway through our first pregnancy, God convicted me of my vanity, so my prayers changed to "God give us the strength to handle whatever you bless us with."

During Missy's pregnancy with Emma, I continued on with that prayer. Ironically, Missy reminded me of those exact words through her tears as we drove back from the hospital at the end of the first day after receiving the news about Emma. She was not blaming me, but was overcome with us tragically experiencing the full breadth of that request.

Another experience came in the form of a reminder as I sat just outside the NICU doors on a bench in the hallway, pondering the initial news of

Emma's heart defect. I received the news from our admitting doctor while Missy had gone home to check on Sadie and gather some clothes. While trying to fathom the dreadful news and wondering how I was going to explain the complexities of it to my wife, a verse began to stir in my mind. Later that morning, while with my two friends, Jeff and Gary, at what was to become our regular lounging area on the second floor of Stanford's Lucile Packard Children's Hospital, I mentioned to them that I was having trouble placing the verse where God takes credit for making His creation with supposed imperfections. After some discussion and searching, we came across the passage that had been stirring in my mind:

> "The LORD said to him, 'Who gave human beings their mouths? Who makes them deaf or mute? Who gives them sight or makes them blind? Is it not I, the LORD?...'"

Exodus 4:11

The scene involves God attempting to motivate a timid Moses who finds himself in an unfamiliar situation and backpedaling from a burning bush into his default mode, while hoping not to head into the new direction God is asking of him. Indirectly, God is making a statement to all of us about His kingdom ways on earth. Specifically, He is saying that disabilities, imperfections, or whatever title you give them are of God and for His purposes. Moreover, what we deem as imperfect could be exactly what He perfectly intended. What we do know is that He creates men and women in His own image and does so in ways unexpected to all of us saturated in the culture of the supposed "perfect look" and other worldly expectations. In the end, Moses was convinced God could not use a man with his clumsy tongue. Likewise, I was in need of convincing that God wanted to use a ten-day-old girl with a sluggish heart.

In the short and long term, God continued to confirm this new perspective beyond my default mode through prayer, song, and other Scriptures. The song "From Above" by Burlap to Cashmere, which I was playing over and over again in those early days, reminded me of who creates us, the blessing of imperfections, the deceptive power of emotions, and how perspective comes from Him above.

My ongoing devotional reading that late spring and early summer in *The Daily Walk Bible* brought forth the following passages about how the life I was brought into was about something greater than myself:

> "…for I have made them for my glory. It was I who created them."
>
> **Isaiah 43:7 (NLT)**

> "Our God is in heaven; he does whatever pleases him."
>
> **Psalm 115:3**

> "The LORD works out everything to its proper end…"
>
> **Proverbs 16:4**

Further study took me to other New Testament passages that paralleled these others.

> "… all things have been created through him and for him."
>
> **Colossians 1:16**

> "God, for whom and through whom everything was made…"
>
> **Hebrews 2:10 (NLT)**

Moreover, the passage, "As for God, his way is perfect," from Psalm 18:30, reconfirmed my faith in God's sovereignty. By sovereignty, I am referring to how God rules with love and concern for us, especially when it does not look or feel like we want it.

the decision

After my sobbing shower, we still had to choose one of the three options as we entered the hospital Friday morning. By mid-afternoon, after more prayer and conversations with others and one final discussion about all the options with Missy, we felt God leading us to attempt to sustain Emma's life by choosing the three-surgery route.

As we discussed our decision with our new cardiologist, Dr. Jeff Feinstein, who had been incredible the day before at being professional, yet compassionate in our initial consultation, we both knew that the Great Physician, God, had brought us through the first stage of this drama. He had guided us with internal (our heart's desire), external (surgical options), biblical (Scripture verses) and communal (others' input and prayer) leadings. In our unfamiliarity, He moved us in faith beyond our fears, selfishness, and convenient desires, into the greater things of God.

The procedure that relieved our tension involved an incision having to be made by God. Upon making the incision, He had to reach into our souls and cut out some of our old, dying perspective and transplant a fresh, new perspective about life being about something greater than ourselves, especially for me. While this invisible procedure left a scar, it provided such great relief.

I believe you will find the rest of the lessons to be a natural outpouring from the perspective gained in this first one.

reflection & challenges

What circumstances in your life (past or current) have caused you to realize that life is about something greater than yourself?

Where does your default mode lead you when faced with unwanted life circumstances?

What holds you back or helps you to include God during the tough times?

Now is the most important time
because it is the only time
when we have any power.

Leo Tolstoy

LESSON TWO

life is (a) short (story)

I T WAS THE FIRST WEEK OF AUGUST 2001, two years and three months after Emma's initial diagnosis and first surgery, as we drove up the road in Vermont to Missy's grandparents' house. It was overcast that early evening, as our car approached their home set in the richness of green grass and trees. I was excited to share our little Sadie and Emma, as well as our newest addition, baby Elise, with them. I knew Missy was too. We never could have believed that, within a month, life as we'd come to know it would be so different.

This was our second stop on a two-week journey. It began with a long flight to Boston. Then a drive to New Hampshire for a five-day stay with my family. My sister, Karen, and her husband, David, hosted my parents and our family at their place on Lake Winnipesaukee. What a fabulous time it had been sharing the grandkids with their grandparents and watching the interaction of the little cousins, all under five years old. Hiking with the kids to Abenaki Tower, ice cream on the sidewalk in Wolfeboro, digging in the sand, being silly on the boat, feeding the baby goats at the local petting farm, playing on the floating dock and watching my nephew, three-year-old Joshua, beg to play the drums in the town square, were just a few of the moments for which we had traveled so far.

Our next stop was Londonderry, Vermont, a one-street town where Missy's grandparents, Jules and Nancy Junker (affectionately known as Grandfather and Mutti), lived. In the late 80s, Missy and I made several road trips here as getaways during college term breaks. The fall was always glorious with the changing leaves; the winter was always frigid; the spring, just muddy; and the summer, thick with humidity and mosquitoes. However, experiencing her grandparents and her extended family of aunts, uncles, and cousins, who all lived locally, overshadowed whatever season we had to enjoy or endure. It was the people that brought us back again and again to this place that had become so special.

As we arrived, the scene was set for a storybook dinner. Imagine if you will, an off-white wooden two-story home, with a green steel roof to fend off the snow, with deeper green shutters. Add a dark red weathered barn just beyond the driveway that wrapped around the house. Off to the side of the barn, the landscape dropped into a wonderful plateau that was perfect for chairs and a wheelbarrow converted into a table, covered with a green and white checked tablecloth set with pewter for a buffet. The kids' table was an oversized log with little chairs next to it. Just out of reach, a few yards below, was the smoking barbecue fire pit, encircled with stacked, flat rocks, where Grandfather tended to the steak and corn.

As we got out of the car, we knew we had to find the camera bag to begin capturing it all. Our two travel-weary towheads shyly emerged from the minivan and met Mutti and also Aimee, Missy's aunt visiting from Nepal. The air was thick with the prospect of rain, but I knew it would hold off, for the outdoor dinner event seemed meant to be.

After the shyness faded, Sadie and Emma found their way to the blueberry bushes that acted as a natural hedge between the dining plateau and the fire pit, while their five-month-old sister, Elise, remained drooling on the front porch strapped in her car seat. Between chasing the cat, looking for bugs, having imaginary conversations at the table, coming too close to the fire, and Emma asking for more and more "bu-berries," the time passed quickly before dinner. Once started, dinner became secondary, as the primary focus became engaging, watching, and commenting on the girls. Filled with pride, I attempted, in the course of twenty minutes, to get them to perform every trick and word they could in order to impress their enraptured audience.

As I walked back and forth from the house while helping to clear the dishes, I was able to take in the moment by just watching and listening. With the evening darkening, the sounds of little girls running and giggling, great-grandparents commenting, and the crickets chirping filling the air, I felt so blessed by God to be there. The screaming minivan ride was worth it, the long flight was worth it, and all the details had been worth it for this one moment. There was something so dear about it, so innocent, so simple, and so beautiful. Maybe it was because one of the most significant places where Missy and I had begun our relationship was colliding with the beginning of our new forming family of five. Or maybe it was because the intensity of the last two years and three months, which included Emma's near death, two surgeries to retrofit her now three-chamber heart, and the birth of sweet Elise was in such stark contrast to the enjoyable calmness of the moment.

In actuality, what seemed like the beginning turned out to be so much closer to the end of Emma's life than I would've ever wanted to realize. Had

I known what the future would hold within the month, I most likely would not have been able to enjoy the moment. But ignorance was truly bliss and if I could live it over and over again, I'd be willing to pay admission.

The next few days were filled with so much joy. The girls were entertained and fussed over by the Junker clan. Creating unique craft projects with Aunt Casey, baking special sweet snacks with Aunt Aimee, exploring the garden and playing on the trampoline with little Aimee (Casey's daughter named after her aunt), and going to the Vermont Country Store filled the spaces between naps and meals. Eleven-year-old little Aimee became the favorite guide of our girls. Her care and concern bonded them deeply to one another in a short period of time. Maybe it was little Aimee's awareness of Emma's condition that made her treat her with such protection and compassion. Or maybe it was just their ages. Either way, it was delightful to watch the connection form.

On the final evening, we had a birthday dinner for Grandfather and me. With fifty years separating us, we ate in the barn to the glow of candlelight with all the local family. The same detailed story about Aunt Casey and Uncle Michael's wedding being held in the barn over fifteen years earlier was told, and I listened to it just like I was hearing it for the first time.

This is why we had come. For the old and new stories of life. There were old stories I heard again about the house, the town, the aunts and uncles when they were younger, plus the experiences that came with moving five kids from Air Force base to Air Force base through three wars. The new stories included an update on the expansion of Uncle Payne and Aunt Elise's iron sculpting/art business, hearing Aunt Aimee speak of the Nepalese culture, taking note of Uncle Michael's explanation of his recent health challenge, and listening to Grandfather detail his computerized mapping project for the local town. The funniest stories were always told by Mutti—her sense of humor was fabulous. And it was so endearing to watch Grandfather listen to her with a sparkle in his eye and chuckle uncontrollably at each story like he had never heard it before. Whether new or old, these short vignettes about their lives enriched me, reflected who God had made them to be, and gave me a window into each of their souls.

the power of a story

Looking back on this final visit to Vermont with Emma, I have learned that life is short and so full of short stories of great value. This became obvious during our stay as I witnessed east and west coast, modern and postmodern, small town and large town, local and global collide in conversation. There, like elsewhere, were a series of people and experiences just waiting to be shared. I didn't mind the repetition of the old stories that were told because they were the significant memorable moments that were embedded in and had shaped the hearts of the individuals and ethos of this surrounding. However, I looked forward to hearing the new or updated stories that added to new chapters and understanding in the lives I had so come to appreciate. Stories are the essence of who people are because they convey where they have come from and where they are headed.

God yearns for us to tell stories, especially the ones that tell of His works. The entire Bible is a collection of this splendor and was intended to pass on the purpose and meaning of life to all. Through Moses, God told the story of the creation and corruption of man. Abraham and Moses were responsible for passing on God's story to the chosen nation of Israel. God went on to use other messengers inside and outside of Israel, known as prophets, to make Himself known to the world. Jesus came as the greatest storyteller of all time, for He was God embodied in a man. God used this more direct means of Jesus to change the course of history in His story. With the crucifixion, death, resurrection, and ascension of Jesus, the followers of God, known as the apostles, were filled with the Holy Spirit and left with the power and position of being God's storytellers. To this day, modern men and women who come to a relationship with God through faith in Jesus are empowered by the Spirit to tell the story of God to all. Those who believe the story and commit to living it out become eternal storytellers. The psalmists conveyed this idea of being storytellers for God:

"Come and hear… let me tell you what he has done for me."

Psalm 66:16

"Let the redeemed of the LORD tell their story..."

Psalm 107:2

I believe the best stories are the ones that involve God. God desires for us to tell our stories from His perspective. Am I saying that all stories without the mentioning of God are wrong? No. I believe God gives us a lot of grace in this area, but He yearns for us to be more reverent in acknowledging who is the Provider and Sustainer of all things. We should be giving the credit where it is due instead of giving credit to ourselves. Most people tell a story and actually believe they accomplished whatever they are subtly boasting about on their own. Meanwhile, the apostle Paul, when attempting to let some of the air out of the puffed-up people of Corinth told them the following:

"... What do you have that you did not receive? And if you did receive it, why do you boast as though you did not?"

1 Corinthians 4:7

Paul wanted them to realize their storytelling and lifestyle was void of God. I desire for people to realize that we are complex human beings living short lives and spinning on a globe that is sustained in an atmosphere by an interested and approachable God. Our stories must involve more than the weather and how much we have accomplished. They must involve God, for we have been birthed into His grand story.

Integrating God into our lives and conversations is possible, for He is in all things and is ever present. That is why He gives His name as "I AM" in Exodus 3:14. "I AM" means the One who is the core of existence and ever present.

As I reflect on the story of our travels to Vermont, my desire is to convey it with an attitude of gratitude because I believe God has made all things possible for us. He ordained my particular short story long before I was even aware of my existence. In this age of individualism, we personalize everything, see things only from our perspective, and feel we deserve everything and anything we want. This is our default mode attempting to blaze our own stories without even considering that there is an actual story designed by God that He wants us to live. The apostle Paul attempted to make this loud and clear in his letter to the church of Ephesus:

> "For we are God's handiwork, created in Christ Jesus to do
> good works, which God prepared in advance for us to do."

Ephesians 2:10

But, you may say, that sounds like enslavement. How could anyone possibly want to submit to someone else having the creative power over the story of one's life? God does not want to enslave us in His story, rather He wants to truly satisfy and partner with us. Should we not be grateful that the One who creates and takes away life has given us the opportunity to partner in His story? He promises peace (John 16:33) and even meeting the desires of our own hearts (Psalm 37:4) for those willing to partner. A follower of Jesus, named John, wrote down Jesus' own words about the abundant life He wants us to experience:

> "The thief comes only to steal and kill and destroy; I have
> come that they may have life, and have it to the full."

John 10:10

Yet the power of culture, combined with our lack of reverence and inner reflection within our default mode keep us from the story that will satisfy and transform us most. Consequently, it is essential that we become deliberate through our thoughts and actions to live out the story with Him and not just on our own.

Story in pictures

As I sat on the plane looking down our row during the flight home from our east coast family adventure, the stark reality of our situation settled back in. We had three children under the age of four. We were outnumbered and so easily overwhelmed. Adding to our reality was that our sweet two-years-and-almost-four-months-old Emma was heading toward her third open heart surgery the first week in September. I don't remember much more about the flight, except that it went from bad to worse when I lost my patience after multiple requests by family members. It resulted in me tugging a backpack under a seat in frustration so hard that it hit sweet Emma in the head as I followed through. That, and the general travel exhaustion, once again, made Missy and I proclaim that we would not return to the East Coast on a flight until our youngest was at least four years old. Fortunately, a few weeks later, on Labor Day weekend, time helped us forget the travel challenges as we looked at photos from our time in Vermont. While reflecting on the adorable and memorable snapshots, we both agreed the family memories made were so worth the effort.

reflection & challenges

Reflect on a scene from your life that God has blessed you with recently or in the past.

Do you believe that your story is a part of God's greater narrative? What has caused this belief or disbelief?

How could you be more open to giving God the credit for the stories you tell?

Wisdom is found in a multitude of counsel.

Unknown

LESSON THREE

let many in

ROUND 8:00 A.M. ON WEDNESDAY, September 5, 2001, Missy and I sat in our usual waiting area at Stanford's Lucile Packard Children's Hospital. It was Emma's third surgery. I had not given much thought as to how the day would play out because just getting to it had taken enough energy. Though we were entering into the third stage of this drama, my mind was still pondering my to-do list and thinking about how I could get it all done.

As Missy and I sat alone on those familiar waiting room couches and I heard the elevator button beep, the power of letting many people in re-entered my mind. I was reminded of how it all had begun two years earlier.

The waiting area had become our living room and the beep of the elevator was like our doorbell. It made me say to Missy, "Should we be expecting anyone to come down besides our parents this time?" She replied, "I think Barb might stop by." I thought to myself, "Yeah, we're veterans. We know this drill." Only Rod Toews, my colleague and executive pastor at our church, had been with us so far on this day. He had faithfully met us at 6:30 a.m. to pray with us and over Emma in the pre-op room. The image of him gently cupping Emma's cheek as he prayed for her just prior to her being released to surgery was a gloriously symbolic foreshadowing of her being placed in the hands of God.

Personally, as I sat there, I kind of hoped that no one else would make such a fuss because I had so many mundane things to do—complete my expense reports, finish reading a book, and figure out how to get my computer fixed. However, on that day, more waves of support came rolling in each time the elevator door beeped and opened. Faces new and old to the drama entered the scene, and what a joy it turned out to be to receive them. Susan and Garrett were some of the unexpected faces. As new friends over the previous two years, we had found our bond in pastoring new flocks of people, our wives having a common Bible study, he and I enjoying barbeque beef lunches, and each having three kids. They exemplified the wave of support—people with busy lives and their own to-do lists. But for some very gracious reason they interrupted their normal routines and made the effort to support us.

How blessed we were! The tiredness and to-do list faded from my mind as we passed the morning laughing, sharing our hearts, updating each other on our lives, and introducing those unfamiliar to each other. For many of us, it was our only point of true connection together in the previous six to eight months.

new lesson, new tension

We cannot take the credit for learning the lesson of letting many in. Letting people into our circumstances wasn't originally our choice. It was forced on us, but it became essential to our survival. At first, I actually attempted to fend off the people. As an extrovert and self-proclaimed control freak, I loved to hang with people, but only on my terms and agenda.

Our friends Brett and Lyn, who are from South Africa, but have lived in the States for decades, have joked that Americans don't do "pop ins." However, in South Africa, folks "pop in" unannounced to see each other and spend a few hours. They found in America that either nobody was home or they would look at you funny when you said, "We're just in the neighborhood and decided to pop in."

"Pop-ins" are my worst nightmare.

Back in May 1999, I found myself getting frustrated as people came down to visit and console us just hours after the news had spread of Emma's diagnosis and hospitalization. Again, it was the unfamiliar that was causing me to want to hole up in my comfortable and well-controlled default mode. Looking back, I guess we had a choice about whether to receive the support or not. I could have sent everyone home and attributed it to the stress and emotional strain. But based on how God flooded us with folks, I don't believe He wanted us to control, hold back, or run from their waves of needed loving support. In His infinite wisdom, He knew that riding these waves with others would keep us from drowning in the undercurrent of emotions that were continually tugging at us and pulling us downward.

learning to ride the waves

Looking back on that frightful morning when it all began on Thursday, May 20, 1999, my friend, Jeff, was the first wave rider that joined us. As I sat alone in shock in the hallway outside the NICU (since Missy had gone back home to attend to our older daughter, Sadie), I felt a hand on my shoulder. As I looked up into his familiar blue eyes and calm smile, he said, "How you doing?" The person and the timing were perfect, which I attribute to God's gracious provision. So often, He provides who we don't even know we need.

During the next two hours, back on that initial day, others began streaming into the hospital. When Missy returned to the hospital, her friend and mentor, Barb, who was a nurse and later became the unofficial caterer throughout Emma's drama, greeted her. In time, thanks to Barb, it became known that if you showed up to visit Emma in the hospital around lunchtime, the food options were spectacular. In addition to her gift of hospitality, the fact that she was a nurse was beneficial, for on that day and in the months to come, my wife had an educated medical friend to consult. I found it divinely amazing how their relationship had begun just a year prior with the intent of Barb mentoring Missy. Again, so often, God provides who we don't even know we need.

I will never forget their initial sobbing embrace. The fact of the matter is that I never saw it, but only heard it. Missy had brought me a change of clothes, so I was stepping into a restroom and closing the door as I heard Barb's voice. The initial cry, "Oh Missy!" was the last thing I heard before the loud weeping muffled by their embrace filled the air. In the bathroom, I looked at my reflection in the mirror as if trying to connect with someone over what I was hearing. I broke into tears of thankful sadness to God as my wife's need and her and Barb's combined painful sorrow collided. It was the beginning of me learning a secondary lesson about letting many in. For it was then that I realized I was not going to be capable of meeting all of Missy's needs during this saga, but God would provide others to help her.

embracing

Although I had only heard their embrace, I witnessed many others throughout and they remain as sweet visuals in my mind. In this day and age of sexual harassment, sexual abuse, and politically correct touch issues, I believe we have distorted the power of physical touch. God yearns for individuals to bless one another with healthy heaps of meaningful touch. How wonderful it was to experience firsthand the comfort and connection expressed through people embracing.

The best man in my wedding, Anthony, received the news about Emma late on that first day because he was tied up working for a Silicon Valley startup company. By the time I greeted him at the doors of the NICU, it was mid-afternoon and he was awash in tears, apologizing for not coming sooner. He shook as we embraced. By that point, I had no tears for him, for I was cried out. I was the one consoling him, already being a six-hour veteran of the journey. The embrace was one of friendship and a common bond of fatherhood.

A day later, in the same hallway, another meaningful embrace took place. Joe, my father-in-law, arrived the day after the initial news. It was Friday around noontime; Barb's "catering" was not fully up and running yet, so we were headed to lunch. As we passed through the doors of the NICU, Joe came around the bend. His wife, Susan, exclaimed in a surprised manner, "Joe!" The previous day, she'd had a very lonely role. She had spent the day retrieving phone calls and holding down our house, all while keeping a happy spirit, entertaining seventeen-month-old Sadie. Joe had only been connected by phone updates like so many others. Their embrace seemed to be a deep release of repressed and unshared emotions of the prior day. The tears shed by both were for their daughter, their granddaughter, themselves, and the reassurance of being together. The moment seemed like minutes. Of all their experiences in marriage, none had been like this one. It was a painfully unique, beautiful moment for them and all of us.

almost missing the Big One

Upon reflecting on the evening of that initial day in May 1999, I realized I almost missed a very rich moment that God had for us. I was getting ready to head back to the hospital after dinner when the phone rang. It was my friend and colleague Gary. He was calling to see if he, his wife, and a group of other couples could come to the hospital that evening to anoint Emma with oil with the hope of healing her heart. The biblical context for this belief comes out of the book of James.

> "Is anyone among you sick? Let them call the elders of the church to pray over them and anoint them with oil in the name of the Lord."
>
> **James 5:14**

I agreed to the event out of spiritual peer pressure. How could I say "no" to my friend and colleague asking to anoint my child with oil? Again, my default mode had taken over. I was in an unfamiliar situation, and I was feeling a ton of tension. My tension stemmed from my lack of having a personal stance on anointing with oil, my lack of faith in healings, my lack of control of how situations had evolved previously that morning, and my general selfish attitude, which was screaming on the inside, "Hey, isn't this

MY daughter's drama? I thought I was the pastor in charge of orchestrating the spiritual events that will surround it!"

Only by God's grace via the urging of my wife and a timely cry in the shower was my default mode avoided. Sadly enough, I almost missed my first glimpse into true unscripted spiritual community because of my unbelief and pride. In hindsight, another secondary lesson of letting people who have faith beyond your own into your circumstances became obvious.

That evening, four couples, along with Missy and I, gathered in a circle and knelt inside a one-room hospital chapel. We called upon God, the Father, to bring healing and/or a world of strength upon us. The room was filled with humility, dependence, and a painful realization that only God could provide whatever was needed for the days to come. After some time, another couple joined us as we headed into the NICU.

The nurses had put up a temporary partition so we could have some "privacy" amongst the other eight babies and as many nurses and doctors in the room. As we gathered around Emma's open, incubator-like bed and began to pray, I watched tears fall from the faces of all present. Some were seeing her for the first time in her condition. A sense of shock, sadness, and sincere desire for God to do something to restore this child brought forth the emotion. I thought to myself, "Oh, how my pride almost made me miss this moment!" As time went on and I experienced additional amazing, divine moments, I would often ponder, "From what else has my default mode of unbelief and pride held me back?"

As my friend, Jeff, anointed Emma with oil, her eyes opened. I had never participated in such a raw form of spiritual community. That evening brought to mind a passage from the Bible.

"Humble yourselves before the Lord, and he will lift you up."

James 4:10

That night, although no dramatic external healing occurred, it made me wonder what healing was happening within me.

lesson confirmed

Two days later, on Saturday, May 22, 1999, Jeff stood next to me in the NICU in the mid-afternoon and said, "It has been good that you have let people in the way you have."

Confused, I replied, "Yeah, I thought the other night was powerful."

He clarified by saying, "I mean that, but also all the events of the last couple days—from all the phone calls taken, to the visitors you have received." I must have looked puzzled, so he continued telling me how it would have been easy for us to hole up and not let friends or family in on the meetings with doctors and the open discussions about our three options.

He stated, "I have seen other couples not let others in, make quick decisions independent of anyone else and then live with the painful consequences." He went on to convey that a shared experience would help to carry us through, regardless of the outcome. Bottom line, he was telling me that being isolated would not be beneficial to us or our friends and family.

lots of waves

The waves of support continued to flow throughout the first year of Emma's life. After her original diagnosis, another friend, Kelley, said she'd tie a piece of pink yarn around her wrist to remind her to pray for Emma while she was away. Soon after, others took the idea further and gave pink yarn to everyone they knew. During that first year, we were forever comforted by seeing people either wearing a pink piece of yarn around their wrist or showing us what they had tied it to as a reminder for them to pray for us.

Our church body, which so wonderfully heaped prayers and meals on us, celebrated with us at Emma's baby dedication that summer, at the three-month mark of her life. In the months that followed, the waves of prayer and meals flowed again and again during Emma's second surgery in September 1999.

The culmination of year one of Emma's life was an overdone, over-attended first birthday party in the backyard of our favorite catering family, Barb and Dave. On that May day in 2000, I remember thinking how ridiculous we were for hosting all these people at our friends' home. No one-year-old, even with Emma's circumstances, should have such a fuss. But in the weeks to come, as I watched the videotape of friends sharing their hearts about Emma, I realized that it was much more than a birthday party. People were celebrating a year-long experience of a life sustained by God. It had the sweet taste of spiritual community that united individuals together to experience something only He could have done.

the drama brings new waves

As I sat with our friends during Emma's third surgery, I pondered, "We haven't hung out with some of these people in over a year." I thought a little deeper and found it odd that the only time I spent time with some of these people was when dramatic events invaded our normal routines. It was a disturbing statement about our lifestyles, yet a wonderful reminder of them reflecting God's love, consistency, and willingness to be there when most needed.

It is intriguing to me how it takes life-and-death situations to draw us together. We so easily forget that the benefits of relationships are there for the taking if we would just engage with each other more in the mundaneness. Sadly enough, I have witnessed those involved with life-and-death situations or major personal struggles isolate themselves due to pride and fear. Again, this is the power of our default mode. But maybe this is God's way of getting our attention. He knows we are incapable of shutting down our agenda. I believe He is attempting to break down our walls of false humility and arrogance, so we let others into the messiness of our fears and troubles. Furthermore, God yearns for us to live life in community:

> "And let us consider how we may spur one another on toward love and good deeds, not giving up meeting together, as some are in the habit of doing, but encouraging one another..."

Hebrews 10:24-25

Although the context of this passage is referring to gathering to worship God and living out a life for Him, the application is the same for us. The writer was telling them they should not do life alone. This "partnering in life" concept is made clearer by the apostle Paul:

> "Carry each other's burdens, and in this way you will fulfill the law of Christ."

Galatians 6:2

One of God's main goals is to have us come together in unity. Yet, we are so desperate to be independent that we will go to the brink of ruin or need to be completely humbled before we will let anyone into our shattered world. This was true in our case. We had to be thrust into a drama to understand how God wants us to be flooded in spiritual community at all times.

Over the next two days, as Emma struggled to recover from her third surgery, there never seemed to be a moment free of friends "popping in." All came with messages of concern and love from spouses and other friends. Some stayed for minutes, others for hours. Food, flowers, teddy bears, balloons, and gifts filled the room. A simple silver charm bracelet with a heart on it from our friends, Chantelle and Buck, was so meaningful to my wife.

We later had it engraved as a memento of the experience and love shown to us. The celebration, concern, educating of visitors, lunches, phone calls, and laughter kept us afloat in the uncharted waters.

the calm before the storm

We needed people more than ever as Emma's situation went from seemingly better, to dreadful, to agonizing as Wednesday afternoon to Friday evening unfolded in September 2001. Arriving back from her third surgery at 12:30 p.m. on Wednesday, September 5, our surgeon informed us at Emma's bedside, as she rested peacefully, that all had gone better than expected. To our delight, at one point in her groggy state, Emma even awoke enough to see Missy and say, "Hi Mama." Yet by Wednesday evening, Missy, panicked with concern, called me at home with the alarming news that Emma had experienced some seizures. Dreadfully, they would not stop. By 2:30 a.m. Thursday morning, Emma was intubated to help her breathe, since stronger medications were needed to stop the seizures. Thursday morphed into a blur of endless tests, more mild seizures, a possible infection, lots of questions, and an unclear plan of action.

entertaining angels

During these confusing and agonizing times, I am astonished how God let in key individuals to our journey who acted as living manifestations of what the Bible tells us about angels:

> "… angels are only servants—spirits sent to care for people who will inherit salvation."
>
> **Hebrews 1:14 (NLT)**

rosalina

On the Wednesday evening of Emma's seizures, Rosalina, the evening nurse, was the first angel who came as a needed voice of truth. After coming to terms with the shock of Emma's seizures as evening turned into morning, I sat up with Emma and Rosalina. She was a lovely Filipina mother, who had several teenage and adult children. We bonded over our situation and faith in God. Her faith taught me an important principle, which she shared with me as I questioned her about the long-term impact of the seizures. It seemed like she was avoiding the question for a while, but then in the near-dawn hours of Thursday, she said to me, "You know these children are not ours. We only get the privilege of caring and experiencing them for the time they have been given to us by God."

Tears rolled down my cheeks as I stroked Emma's arm and repeated the statement, "We only get the privilege of caring and experiencing them for the time…" After a while, I fully received and accepted this unfamiliar statement.

The next time she entered the room I replied with a sigh, "You are right, Rosalina." I felt an odd sense of peace and fear from her loving words of comfort. That morning, as Emma's condition worsened, we were blessed that Rosalina was willing to extend her shift to eighteen hours when her relief called in sick.

steve

As Friday morning came around, it seemed to bring some stability to Emma's body and mind, though the extent of the damage from the seizures was still unknown. Around noon, as I drove down to the hospital to relieve Missy, hope and peace arose in me from listening to a voicemail left late the previous night by my Tennessee friend, Steve. Steve had prayed for me with the words of Paul to have peace beyond all understanding:

"Do not be anxious about anything, but in every situation, by prayer and petition, with thanksgiving, present your requests to God. And the peace of God, which transcends all understanding, will guard your hearts and your minds in Christ Jesus."

Philippians 4:6-7

In the moment, I was fortunate enough to be living out the blessings of this concept, which gave me perspective for the unknown events that were ahead of us. I chuckled to myself, for Steve had always been a zealous prayer warrior with an admirable faith. Once again, his gift of faith was inspiring me as it had in the past. Steve had been used like an angel with the right message at the right time to help soothe my soul.

allison

After listening to that voicemail in my car, I re-entered Emma's room on Friday, September 7, kissed my wife, and relieved her for lunch. Based on all the gifts in the room, I concluded that the pop-in traffic had been heavy. I introduced myself to the nurse overseeing Emma's care. Her name was Allison. As usual, the first thing I did was begin my gracious inquiry. After a few questions, I was grateful that she seemed so compassionate and competent. Plus, it was fun to hear about her marriage, their recent move, and her engagement in a local church.

The rotating nursing staff was no longer just a group of attendants to my daughter that changed every twelve hours. Over the previous two years, these providers of care had become an intimate part of our lives and an angelic source of encouragement, both medically and spiritually.

tony

By Friday afternoon, with Allison attentively present, pop-in traffic heavy, and Emma's condition less critical, things seemed more hopeful. Around 3:00 p.m., my friend and colleague in ministry, Tony, showed up in the atrium area outside the PICU, as I was saying goodbye to some others.

There I said to Tony, "Hey, you didn't have to come down. You were just here yesterday afternoon." He agreed, but explained that he had been out late the night before doing college ministry, and upon waking up, he felt God telling him to go to the hospital. It was his day off, so he decided to run some errands and then stop by. Knowing and envying his spiritual discernment, I thanked him for listening to God and invited him to come into the room to see Emma.

Tony had a way of popping into my life at the most unexpected times. We first met in the spring of 1997 as roommates in a house in the Colorado mountains. Through our denomination, we had both been placed on a team that had come together to plan a week-long national Christian college student summer experience. During those four days, I grew to admire this young college student of faith who was my opposite in many ways. He was from Chicago and into drama, earrings, dressing hip, swing dancing, creative thinking, coloring his hair, and the mystical, expressive aspect of God. Meanwhile, I was from Pittsburgh and into sports, dressing preppy, thinking logically, and the contemplative, more reserved aspect of God.

During that stay together in Colorado, my sister, Karen, called, rattled and heartbroken over a recent miscarriage. Being trapped in the mountains of Colorado and not being able to support her more was very disappointing to me. Tony listened and prayed for me and my sister's situation. I was amazed by his mature and compassionate heart as a college student. Within the next year, after his graduation, we invited him to join our pastoral staff to work with college students.

In the years that followed, God went on to bless me and our church with Tony's outside-the-box, expressive, and passionate Christian faith. The more time I spent with him, the more I knew I needed him around me to help me grow in ways that were unfamiliar.

all angels on deck

As Tony and I entered Emma's room, Allison was scurrying about having just returned from her lunch break. The break nurse, Paula, was updating Allison on the last hour of care. As I explained Emma's current condition to Tony, I watched as Allison checked the reactiveness of Emma's pupils. Just prior to breaking for lunch, Allison and I had had a conversation regarding Emma's pupils being a bit sluggish when the flashlight was shined in her eyes. Allison assured me it was the anti-seizure medication that made her pupil reflexes sluggish. I thought nothing of it until I happened to see Allison with her little flashlight walk towards Emma again. I remember saying, "I will be interested to see if they are still so sluggish," as I took a few steps towards the bed to get a closer view.

As Allison lifted Emma's eyelid, I was shocked by how much of her pupil I saw. In my mind I thought it odd that I could barely see a rim of blue around the edges of the oversized pupil. I noticed that as she shone the light in Emma's eye, the pupil did not move at all. She did it again and the result was the same. I had no idea what that meant medically, but the tension in me increased as the other eye mimicked the first.

Instantly I said sternly, "Allison, what does this mean?"

She turned and looked at me, and I saw the fear of death in her eyes. Her response was, "I have to get a doctor."

The look in her eyes was unforgettable, a combination of sadness and shock. It seemed like she wanted to cry and/or scream. Her eyes quickly left mine as she headed out the door to find a doctor. As the doctor came into our room and leaned over Emma's bed, my wife returned. Our angel of the moment, Tony, was prayerfully pacing in the far corner of the room and leafing through Scripture, as I had seen him do many times. For the next two hours, this obedient angel, Tony, who had listened to the simple nudge of God to join us in this moment, became our wave of support.

Within a minute or two, after watching the medical team that had stormed the room and frantically pulled all the plugs from the wall, we became a moving roadshow, headed for an emergency brain scan, with six people attending to Emma's heavily equipped mobile bed as we chased with Tony trailing closely behind. It was like a scene from some emergency room television show. The searing reality was that we were that family chasing the rushing bed instead of being outside observers watching a fictional drama unfold from the safety of our couch.

Looking out from our fast-moving scene, all I could see were the eyes of rubbernecking doctors, nurses, attendants, patients, and their families, catching a quick glance of us as we rolled at a panic-stricken pace through the unit. We had been in their shoes prior, watching others stream by as we remained stationary, shocked, and wondering, "Wow, something really bad is going on with that family. What could it be?" But now, it was us.

As the doors of the CAT scan lab swung closed, Missy and I entered a vacant conference room that was adjacent and lit only by the light of the hallway. She crumpled to the ground in tears beneath a whiteboard, praying out loud to God, and I paced around the conference room table, holding and rubbing my forehead with both hands, lost in the quandary of what God was doing. As I looked out to find Tony, I saw faith again. His body was postured as the letter X with his hands spread high on the doors of the CAT scan lab praying to God.

In time, Emma's mobile bed burst back out of the lab and our chase ensued. This time, the pace was slower—a quick walk instead of a dash. The adrenaline had decreased and the tears were dried up. The piercing thoughts of losing our daughter were penetrating. It was unfamiliar. Shock and disbelief were our staple emotions, and questions filled our hallway conversation.

more waves still needed

After Emma's roadshow settled back into her room around 5:30 p.m. that Friday evening, five doctors stood at the end of the bed as my wife and I, our parents, Tony, our senior pastor, Jon, and Barb encircled Emma as she lay there. They conveyed to us the news we had been dreading for two hours.

"Mr. and Mrs. Rhen, your daughter is brain dead," said the head of the PICU. After explaining our limited options, the doctors began to leave the room to give us space. I requested that our cardiologist, Dr. Jeff Feinstein, stay with us. At that point, I felt all we could do was join hands and pray for wisdom. After praying, we asked for each person to give us his or her opinion of what we should do. Looking back, it was not a fair question to ask. Only the child's parents can really make that decision and live with it. However, the Bible does tell us that there is a multitude of wisdom in the counsel of many and that was what we were searching for.

With no concise leading from the group, our options seemed to be either to wait for a miracle or release sweet little Emma off the breathing machine. So, Missy and I headed out for a walk to have the toughest discussion of our lives. We had no idea that over the next several crucial hours even more people would be let in, giving shape to God's direction and the other lessons learned in this journey.

reflection & challenges

What challenging circumstances in your life (past or current) have caused you to let many in?

What have been the benefits of letting others in?

What have been the consequences of not letting others in?

For every movement of God,
there is a causal factor
either prompted by
good or evil.

Dr. Joe Roberson
Former Chief of
Otology-Neurotology-Skull Base Surgery
Stanford University

LESSON FOUR

life is out of our control

J UST AFTER 5:30 P.M. ON FRIDAY, September 7, 2001, Missy and I walked
out of Emma's room and headed down the hall, realizing we needed to
call home. Earlier, in the midst of the chaos surrounding Emma's rapid
decline, I managed to make a call to Wendy, a friend and one of Sadie's
favorite babysitters. Fortunately, I caught her on her cell phone while she
was closing up her second grade classroom for the weekend. With limited
explanation so as not to overwhelm her, I asked her if she could go relieve
my mom and dad at our house so they could come down to the hospital
immediately. She agreed without hesitation and got her friend and our other
favorite sitter, Erin, to join her. These two women were our "dynamic duo"

with our girls. We never thought their loyalty and willingness to serve us would prove to be so valuable for our entire family.

Once down the hall, we called again to let them know the situation might last through the night. As it turned out, Tony had been calling them with hourly updates of Emma's condition. To know the information they knew and to still be able to care for six-month-old Elise and almost-four-year-old Sadie, truly showed their strong character and amazing reliance on God in a time of deep despair.

a familiar face in an unfamiliar place

As I hung up the phone and we began to walk down the hall toward an outdoor sitting area on the second floor, a surprising, familiar face came around the corner. It was Francisco, a sixteen-year-old from East Palo Alto, CA, who taught tennis to kids at the Community Center associated with our church. Francisco and I had always exchanged pleasantries and had a few incidental conversations, but nothing more. That was about to change.

I asked him why he was there, and he informed us that his aunt had gone into labor when he was in the car with her and another family member. If his afternoon experience with his aunt had not been shocking enough, I then explained to him that my wife and I needed to step outside to have a crucial conversation about our daughter who was in the hospital. As we parted, I assumed I would not see him again.

Once outside, Missy and I sat down on a bench, and I realized this was not going to be an easy conversation. Within seconds, it was obvious to each of us what the other thought regarding the next step with Emma. Unfortunately, we did not have similar opinions. I felt the need to wait and see what could happen. My gut wanted to get other people down to the hospital. It just felt right. Meanwhile, Missy was questioning the purpose of waiting and delaying the inevitable. The doctors had told us that this condition was most likely irreversible. Brain dead was brain dead. Since she could not breathe on her own, letting her go seemed like the rational thing to do. So, there we sat—stuck—and at that moment, I noticed Francisco standing at the door to the patio, trying to figure out how to open it.

I opened the door to help Francisco get outside onto the patio. As he sat down next to us, he asked the question that would connect the three of us for the rest of our lives.

"So what are you guys doing here?"

A bit sarcastically, I answered, "Francisco, that is an interesting question and I am sorry that the answer will scar you for the rest of your life, but God must want it this way." We had just prayed for wisdom and direction in Emma's room and the bizarreness of this "divine appointment" made me believe that there must be wisdom to be found in it.

Turning to him and looking directly at his profile as he sat next to me, I quickly gave him Emma's medical history and explained her current condition. Then I ended by saying, "So that is our story; that is why we sit here. We are trying to determine when and if we should take our daughter off life support."

I finished by asking him an unfair question. "Francisco, what do you think we should do?" Without hesitation, this sixteen-year-old, who had not looked me in the eye during my entire explanation to his initial question, turned and seemed to stare into my soul with his dark brown eyes and replied, "Keep trying."

an unfamiliar question

After absorbing his words, I turned to Missy, raising my open hands above my head to the sky in amazement with a half-nervous laugh and stated, "Honey, did you hear what Francisco said? He said that we should keep trying." My wife seemed to have a non-reaction to either my comment or his, but then joined the conversation with the most unexpected question of all. Within seconds of finishing my statement, she said to him, "Francisco, are you a Christian?"

I knew things were totally out of human control at this point, because my wife is not an evangelist and neither am I. The question was not a natural one for her to ask, and it seemed out of place and irrelevant to the situation. With Missy leading us into unfamiliar territory, I just followed along. As I was listening to Francisco explain his nominal Catholic background, his battles with epilepsy, and his yearning for more in life, I was simultaneously telling God how ridiculous this all was. In my mind, I was saying, "God, you have got to be kidding me. You want me to explain to this kid how my faith in Jesus has given me access to Your perspective and peace in the midst of our drama, so he can experience it in his own life? No, God, this isn't really happening, is it?"

After asking some clarifying questions and listening to his responses, I began to tell Francisco what it really meant to be a Christian. I told him how it was not about what kind of church you go to or what you do for a living. It was about humbling yourself enough to have a daily relationship with God. I explained that God, the Creator of this world, made him, loves him, yearns to have a relationship with him and has plans for him. I conveyed we are not capable on our own of determining our purpose on this earth, of freeing ourselves from the shame of our sinfulness, or of receiving a true sense of peace, contentment, and perspective apart from a personal relationship with God. I clarified how Jesus came to earth to be sacrificed for us so that our sinfulness could be forgiven and then we could be in constant relationship with God the Father through the Holy Spirit.

After my explanation, Francisco had some clarifying questions. I then asked him, "Francisco, would you like me to tell you more about Jesus or would you like to go so Missy and I can finish our conversation?" He remained and asked more questions. Two more times I asked him a similar question, giving him the opportunity to go. Only after telling him more about Jesus the third time, did I then move to some sort of closure, for we had a decision to make and so did he. My intent was not to push him, but to honor the divine situation God had us in.

I hesitantly said to Francisco, "Before you go, I would like to give you the opportunity to begin a relationship with God by putting your faith in Jesus. I am going to pray a prayer to help you do that, and if all this has made sense and you desire to begin this relationship, then you can pray it silently." As I shifted my body to pray, Francisco removed his hat. My prayer was simple, and he remained silent.

As Francisco stood up to leave, I told him that in some crazy way he may have been an answer to our prayers and that I would follow up with him at a later date. And then he left.

Missy and I looked at each other in a disbelieving, smirking, head-shaking kind of way. What had just happened? We thought we were just going to make the biggest decision of our lives, but a teen's spiritual life took center stage over the issue of Emma's life support. Or did it? Was God just reminding us that, as the Creator, He is present with us as He brings about life and death within souls simultaneously? Obviously, we believed it was a sign from God.

After a brief conversation, we agreed to "keep trying." This would involve talking to the doctors more, gathering our friends and family around us, and seeing what would happen as we waited. Some might say we were grasping for any option other than taking control and releasing Emma, while others might argue that we were following the leadings of God. All I really knew was that a sixteen-year-old (who had appeared out of nowhere) had brought unity to a couple seeking their way out of misery after praying for wisdom.

As we left the patio, I pondered the fact that over the span of just a few hours, a baby had been born, a child had gone brain dead, and a young man had possibly been born again. Life was definitely out of our control.

lesson confirmed—I told you there would be trouble

Sitting with Francisco had not been in our plan for that day. Friday was the day we were supposed to be walking the halls with a recovering Emma, the Stanford Children's Hospital "poster child" for Hypoplastic Left Heart Syndrome. Instead, I was walking and sitting with Tony, Francisco, and others not scheduled in my calendar, but with whom I was apparently supposed to have divine appointments.

From her seventh day of life, Emma had been teaching us that life was out of our control and not about our agenda. We believed that in theory, yet often acted in the contrary. Two verses, from John 16 and Psalm 115, were key to re-educating us about control during our short walk with Emma.

The first is the conclusion of a greater dialogue that is worth understanding.

> "I have told you these things, so that in me you may have
> peace. In this world you will have trouble. But take heart! I
> have overcome the world."

John 16:33

In John 16:33, which I call the "I told you there would be trouble" passage, Jesus has just finished laying out to His disciples the news of His deathly departure and return to God, the Father. From chapters fourteen through sixteen, He uses the phrase, "I have told you," five different times to emphasize His point. In John 14, Jesus begins the dialogue, with the intent to comfort His disciples about the unknown and unfamiliar future that is ahead of them. He tells them to trust in God and in Him, for He and the Father are one and that no one can come to God except through Him. He tells them that God, the Father, will send a Counselor, the Holy Spirit, sometime after Jesus exits the world, who will teach and remind them forever of the things He has said to them. And He promises them peace:

"Peace I leave with you; my peace I give to you. I do not give to you as the world gives. Do not let your hearts be troubled and do not be afraid."

John 14:27

He does not want them to be distressed by the unfamiliar future before them, but instead yearns for them to be dependent on God the Father, through the wisdom of the Holy Spirit and Jesus's example. He wants them to believe Him and conveys this with the first of the five "I have told you" statements:

"I have told you now before it happens, so that when it does happen you will believe."

John 14:29

Jesus continues to remind them of how much God loves them and wants to bless them with the second "I have told you" statement:

"I have told you this so that my joy may be in you and that your joy may be complete."

John 15:11

In the beginning of John 16, Jesus gives another reason for why He is telling them all these things with the third "I have told you" statement:

"All this I have told you so that you will not fall away."

John 16:1

He continues to tell them how they will face persecution, even to the point of death, by those who do not know the Father. Wanting them to believe Him and have peace as the unfamiliar approaches, He makes His fourth "I have told you" statement:

"I have told you this, so that when their time comes you will remember that I warned you about them."

John 16:4

Jesus continues in John 16 to reassure them that the Holy Spirit will be a guide for them after He is gone. In their state of grief and confusion over this surprising news of His impending departure, He tells them that, in time, their grief will turn into joy, specifically when they meet again in heaven. For the first time, the disciples seem to get it. They claim:

"Now we can see that you know all things… This makes us believe that you came from God."

John 16:30

Elated by their deepened belief, Jesus quickly reminds them about the coming time when they will scatter and leave Him. He consoles them by telling them that He will not be alone, for the Father will be with Him. He ends this dialogue with His fifth and final "I told you" statement, which conveys clearly the reality of this world and a reassurance of His power and peace for those who live in it.

"I have told you these things, so that in me you may have peace. In this world you will have trouble. But take heart! I have overcome the world."

John 16:33

Just like Jesus was trying to tell them in chapter fourteen that they could have peace, He restates it in chapter sixteen after clarifying what all the trouble will look like. For the disciples, persecution from others and personal doubt would be their robbers of peace. For us, who live in the first world of the West and who lack true physical persecution, I believe personal discomfort and doubt act as the thieves of our peace.

Many blame God for the trouble in the world. Their opinion is that God should do something about all the poverty, crime, and disease. Most assume He does not really care, since all this trouble goes on within His beautiful creation. But God does care. He loves us so much that He has given us enough freedom to choose to follow His ways, while giving us the same freedom to not. I am not saying that those who do not follow His ways end up committing all the evil in this world. Even those of us who attempt to follow His ways cause evil in this world.

The root cause is that men and women, while made in the image of God, inherited an imperfect strand of sinful tendencies into our imperfect bodies, which makes us susceptible to sin and disease. Consequently, much of the trouble you see in the world today is a result of men and women's default modes spinning out of control. And much of the disease is caused indirectly by either consequences of man's actions or directly by our imperfect bodies. The result is that we find ourselves as fallen people in a fallen world.

While we know our bodies and this world are broken, we still yearn for answers and/or some sense of relief. Answers are not always there, for much of life is a mystery and out of our control, but there is the potential to experience peace even without answers.

While we received some answers to the bigger questions that came our way in the course of Emma's drama, we received much more tangible relief in the form of peace from God than answers. There was no answer to the cause of the seizures Emma began to have on the night after her surgery. Was it a health professional error, her flawed body, or God-initiated? And we still don't know how or why the infection began.

However, we do know that in the midst of the painful troubles, we felt peace in the moments. Peace enough for me to hold our crying surgeon in my arms and tell him he is a good man even though Emma's recovery had gone bad. Peace enough to feel burdened for Allison, our nurse, who lives with the vision of Emma's over-dilated pupils. Her trauma from that moment was so real and so deep that as I hugged her in the hallway after the CAT scan, she cried and said, "We are the ones supposed to be helping you, not you helping us."

It was not that we were without pain or confusion on that day, but we were given a unique sense of peaceful perspective, knowing God was in control. This enabled us to be void of panic. And that is what Jesus has promised for all of us in this out-of-our-control world.

The second verse that exposed us to the reality of life being out of our control speaks to God's role in it.

"Our God is in heaven; he does whatever pleases him."

Psalm 115:3

I remember the date I came across this passage. It was June 15, 1999 (roughly one month after Emma's birth and diagnosis). Reading this passage gave me understanding of past events in our life and some that were yet to come. Further study took me to other passages that reconfirmed that God is the one in charge.

"The LORD does whatever pleases him, in the heavens and on the earth, in the seas and all their depths."

Psalm 135:6

"The LORD works out everything to its proper end—even the wicked for a day of disaster."

Proverbs 16:4

"The Lord will fulfill his purpose for me..."

Psalm 138:8 (RSV)

Simply put, these remind me that the Creator of this Universe, God, put us on this earth for His purposes, not our own. It begins with remembering that we live on a tilted, revolving earth that stays steady in an atmosphere beyond our own doing. Take it one step further and you have to be foolish to think that this was all created so that you can get an education, a great job, a little fame, and sock enough money away as soon as possible so you can start living a comfortable, trouble-free life.

Actually, one very good reminder for me to cut through my personal delusion comes from King David who had a true heart for God:

"As for God, his way is perfect..."

Psalm 18:30

It seems the more I experience what is pleasing to God, which are His perfect ways, the more I experience peace, contentment, and true satisfaction, even when these things have come through pain. Many times, what I have wanted has not been of God's will. Yet, the outcome, though out of my control and usually the result of a very painful process, tends to be something I never could've dreamed of. It's kind of like wanting to get from point A to B in life, but realizing through His guiding hand that you actually ended up at C. I have found location C to be so much better than I could have ever imagined B would be.

For example, upon graduating from college, I thought I wanted to be a pharmaceutical sales representative. My default mode had me convinced this job was "making it big," coming out of the East Coast, white, suburban, wannabe-Ivy-League college life I grew up in. After overcoming a lacking GPA and a brutal round of interviews, a broken de-icing machine at a rural airport in Pennsylvania kept me from getting to the final interview day. However, those out-of-my-control circumstances gave me an opportunity to interview for another job, which relocated me to the West Coast and was the beginning of an array of events that led my faith to awaken. If I had stayed on the East Coast, I believe my insecurities, the familiarity, and the culture would've continued to stagnate my faith. Don't get me wrong: I am not against the background I came from, nor the school I attended, nor being a pharmaceutical sales representative, nor the East Coast. Actually, I do believe that God has used all of it for good to get me to the exact place I am. As for God, His ways do seem perfect, for C was much better than B would have been for me.

The apostle Paul was a well-schooled Jew with a pedigree that was used by God to educate the Jews and the world about Christ. And while I am not saying that I was half as well-schooled as Paul, I do agree with what he tells us:

> "And we know that God causes everything to work together
> for the good of those who love God and are called according
> to his purpose for them."

> **Romans 8:28 (NLT)**

This passage promises us that the out-of-control things in our lives will be used by God and even make sense when we fall humbly in love with Him and His ways. Oh, how the Creator of all yearns to realign the scattered cards of our un-shuffled decks into a purposeful pile!

Specifically regarding Emma's situation, we have found this promise to be true. Missy and I always desired to leave California so we could afford to buy a house. However, a calling into vocational ministry and seminary for a master's degree totally redirected our plans to leave the state. In hindsight, we ended up in the best place medically and spiritually when it came time for Emma's birth and dealing with her needs. We were frustrated when we had to leave our current group health insurance plan and join another, which required switching from a smaller local community hospital to the larger Stanford Hospital. However, because of our new familiarity with Stanford Hospital, it was logical to take Emma there when she ran into trouble that early morning, seven days after her birth. Stanford is one of the few emergency rooms that has pediatric doctors on call at all times, which was vital to stabilizing her that first night. God's ways are perfect even when life seems out of control.

I could go on and on, conveying story after story about how God does whatever pleases Him and how He will intervene in our lives. Though, we most likely receive these divine interventions as "inconvenient," if we stop and ask what is really going on, we will be comforted, gain perspective, and be given direction from Him. In our family, "inconvenient divine interventions" have come in all different forms. However, the common theme in all of these events is that God has worked out everything for His own ends and our good even though these events have seemed unfair and out of our control.

walking back into reality

With our recent experience with Francisco and God's perspective, Missy and I walked back down the hall to proclaim our "keep trying" decision to our family, friends, and doctors. A mixture of an underlying peaceful gratitude and a growing deep sadness swirled within us. The peaceful gratitude stemmed from how clearly God had conveyed our next step with Emma and the growing sadness from the seemingly bleak, unknown hours before us. The second floor of the hospital where celebration (Labor & Delivery) and crisis (PICU) met each day seemed to mimic our emotional state.

reflection & challenges

What do you think about the idea that this life is not ours to control, but is about being led by God?

When life is out of control, how do you find peace?

How might God be leading you through seemingly uncontrollable circumstances and wanting you to hold onto His perspective?

Life and death,
Joy and sorrow,
Pleasure and pain,
Can and do coexist.
Embrace them both.
Don't wait.
Live in the paradox.
Make peace with the mystery.
For He is Lord over it all and He loves you.

Kristin Overton
a mother, friend, and counselor

LESSON FIVE

let circumstances shape you

AS I STOOD IN EMMA'S HOSPITAL ROOM around dinner time on September 7, 2001, facing some of my closest family and friends, who were positioned in an imperfect horseshoe around Emma's bed, I could feel my heart racing as I began to speak. I thought to myself, "Why is this so hard?" Glancing into my wife's eyes next to me, I was wondering if she was feeling the same way.

It was as if the foundational peace beneath us was beginning to shake and crumble. Hadn't I just experienced God's leadings in such a unique and obvious manner out on the hospital patio with Francisco? Hadn't I spoken deep declarations in front of hundreds of people at wedding celebrations, baby dedications, memorials, public assemblies, seminars and weekly church gatherings?

The unfamiliar was driving my fear and causing my peace to erode. Furthermore, I had no mental model for this situation. Never before had I publicly conveyed my deepest convictions on the issue of life support. As parents, we'd never had to face a decision of this magnitude.

Frankly, I couldn't believe how scared I was, despite being surrounded by all the people who cared the most for me and my family. At the time, I couldn't pinpoint the real reason for my fear. Was it my default mode yearning for the approval of others, coupled with the angst of handling their potential contrary views? I believe my trepidation was fueled by the fear of somehow missing out on what God truly wanted us to do. What if we had fooled ourselves into believing that "waiting and seeing" was the right choice?

In my mind, I reviewed the process. We had prayed as a group for wisdom and direction after learning of Emma's dreadful condition. We had asked for counsel from friends and family. Missy and I then stepped away in order to come to common ground on our next step. Upon realizing our differing opinions on the issue, we had the divinely bizarre experience with Francisco who told us to "keep trying." These experiences shaped and formed our united front. My original (and I believe, divine) nudge to "wait " had been confirmed. So as the words came out of my mouth hesitantly and filled with fear, I stood on those leadings from God that seemed like moorings not quite set in the cement of my soul.

As I began to explain our decision to "wait and see" to everyone in the room, I did not mention our experience with Francisco. It was so outside the box, complicated, and bizarre. In reflection, I regret not sharing it. Doing so would have helped us explain our hearts, shown God's powerful movement and presence, and given Him more of the credit. My fearful default mode overrode the sharing of that divine moment.

Instead, I thanked everyone for their support and acknowledged the potential differences of opinion. I expressed that in twenty years, I hoped not to regret this day by wishing we had done something differently (and I didn't). Logically, I told them that it appeared there was no harm in "waiting and seeing." Things had happened so quickly that we were not ready to turn off the respirator, end Emma's life, and just go home. Spiritually, I explained that it seemed there was more to be done by God, although I did not know what that was. I conveyed that I did not know how long we would wait; however, we would begin some discussions with the doctors, contact other family members, and invite other local friends to the hospital.

Our decision was well received with only silent nods of agreement. In many ways, it seemed like a cruel parental initiation rite. It was a decision only we could make. The power, responsibility, and outcome was ours to hold. It was the most lonely place to be as a mother and father. We didn't want to be the "Mr. and Mrs. Rhen" who had to make the call. Yet, how grateful I was for God's obvious presence and leadings that gave direction and courage in the face of those most unwanted circumstances.

Shaped by broken circumstances

Looking back, I believe our circumstances over the two previous years had shaped and molded us in preparation to make that decision on that September day in 2001.

Back on July 4, 1999, we had already hit bottom once with Emma's situation. As fireworks exploded high in the sky off in the distance, our life felt as if it were imploding. My parents were in town and sitting in our living room, making our master bathroom the best place for us to have privacy and a good fight. Missy and I were extremely irritated with each other. The day itself had not met our expectations, nor had we for each other. We were running on empty, lost in the depth of the reality of Emma's illness, and she was only just shy of two months old.

Since her arrival home from surgery a month prior, adrenaline had sustained us. Missy played the role of the ultimate caregiver, and I, an optimistic juggler of tasks. However, with the arrival of July, I watched my wife grow weary, and I had become overwhelmed with all the responsibilities of home, ministry, and seminary schooling, not to mention the loss of private time to recharge. Plus, in the prior two months, we'd had no time for each other. Life had consisted of caring for Sadie, our 18-month-old, and overseeing the maintenance (feeding tube, sleeping issues, endless doctor visits, and health concerns) of sweet baby Emma recovering from her first heart surgery. Meanwhile, Missy was also recovering from having just given birth six weeks earlier. Bottom line—we were physically, emotionally, spiritually, and relationally empty. Or as author Ruth Haley Barton puts it—dangerously tired.[6]

So, as we argued in the master bathroom about things I cannot even remember and cried about the overwhelming circumstances, we both came to the realization that we did not have the strength or wisdom to deal with our situation. There seemed to be no end in sight and no solution. So much frustration, sadness, blame, unacknowledged grief, anxiety, and fear filled that small space we resided in. For the first time, we both simultaneously hit rock bottom. In the past, one of us would sustain the other with rational reasoning or emotional hope, but on this night, neither could. We came to the realization that God's strength was our only option.

Though humility turned us to God that night, our short prayer time did not seem adequate for two people so desperate for answers. My default mode was misrepresenting what God expected of us in our brokenness. I assumed we had to lie on that floor for two days and fast for Him to hear us. On the contrary, a simple prayer in the midst of our crushing circumstances was all that it took to begin shaping and strengthening us in new ways.

Over time, our brokenness continually drove us to God. Circumstances with Emma, especially her fussiness, sleeplessness, endless maintenance, and potentially hopeless future continually forced us into becoming God-dependent people. By God-dependent, I mean going to Him about the littlest and biggest things of life. We still experienced nights of being overwhelmed and angry. Many more, in fact. But, we never had another night like that one. God used that night to help us realize that He allows our circumstances to shape us.

lesson confirmed

The shape that God yearns to mold us into is His likeness. Do you believe that? That He really is the potter and we are the clay? I do believe that and I am grateful to be the clay. Yet, I am most amazed how we are so unwilling to be the clay and how much we desire to be the potter. The funny part is that when we act like the Creator, we have no idea what to do with the clay. Remember the first time you ever tried a potting wheel? The best you could do was let the wet clay run through your hands or make tall hollow spinning towers that would flop down in seconds, or possibly twirl a blob of something no one else could recognize. But when the clay gets in the hands of the One who knows the right mixtures and has the right touch, remarkable things happen.

Still, I am convinced that we all want and try to be the Creator at times, so we can shape our futures and get all the credit. Again, this is all part of our default mode. We get angry or bitter or frustrated when circumstances come spinning into our paths and attempt to knock us off our wheel. We want to control, determine, conquer, and receive all the glory. In most cases, acting as the Creator leads only to isolation and anxiety. Without the Creator, we end up either big-headed with pride from our success, or bitter with pain from our failure. Meanwhile, the Creator is willing to partner with us to meet the desires of our heart, walking us through the difficult circumstances and providing peace, all while spinning everything together so that we are transformed into something that is a magnificent manifestation of Him.

Need something a little more tangible to understand this partnership between Creator, clay and circumstance? Take for example, my friend, Nate. The son of a United States diplomat in the Foreign Service, he was raised in Europe, but finished his high school years back in the States on the East Coast. He was raised to achieve and succeed through his own humanistic efforts, like so many of us. His hard work combined with his God-given intelligence led to a Dartmouth degree and a masters from Stanford in mechanical engineering. A fulfilling job was easily accessible in his desired field of designing biomedical equipment. Then 9/11 struck, and he did not have a box or an answer for the evil in the world. Prior to this point, he had been the molder of his own clay. However, the overwhelming, spinning circumstances brought an end to his self-reliance and an openness to the help of the Creator.

His uneasiness and questions surrounding the incomprehensible evil actions of 9/11 became the gateway through which Nate entered into the crucible that began to shape him internally and externally into a reflection of God. Pastorally, I had never met someone so humble and brilliant that was so open to the molding of God. I witnessed him allow the Potter to form him more and more as he engaged in His Word, prayer, spiritual community, worship, and living out His kingdom perspective of service, integrity, and love in his daily life and work. In time, after receiving the gift of his wife and settling into marriage, life circumstances became daunting due to a medical crisis and his parents' sudden empty-nest divorce. This time, as the wheel of life spun out of control, he allowed the hands of the Potter to hold and mold him. Though it was painful, he found perspective and peace in the hands of the Potter.

Oh, how the Creator wants to shape us into His likeness through the circumstances of our lives! Not many understand or even believe that this is the actual intent of God. The Creator has created us, both men and women, in His image for His glory.

> "So God created mankind in his own image, in the image of God he created them; male and female he created them."
>
> **Genesis 1:27**

> "…everyone who is called by my name, whom I created for my glory, whom I formed and made."
>
> **Isaiah 43:7**

Though these passages make it clear, the lack of faith in Scripture and the default mode of mankind has splintered this mission of God into multiple religions, each with its own traditions and great divisions. Furthermore, religions with traditions have reduced a relationship with God into a rule-based approach of legalism. Legalism leads to pride or shame, which manifests into everything from war to isolation. How quickly we have forgotten that the original intent of God was to create men and women into His masterpieces for His preordained purposes as clarified by the apostle Paul, who was a very capable humanist prior to the Lord intervening in his life:

> "For we are God's handiwork, created in Christ Jesus to do good works, which God prepared in advance for us to do."
>
> **Ephesians 2:10**

The wonderful part is that when we align properly with the Creator, we will find delight and our deepest desires will be met as stated in this Psalm:

> "Take delight in the LORD, and he will give you the desires of your heart."
>
> **Psalm 37:4**

In the same vein, the prophet Isaiah, who was a mouthpiece for God, warned us against wanting to become the Creator and not being willing to be formed by Him:

> "What sorrow awaits those who argue with their Creator. Does a clay pot argue with its maker? Does the clay dispute with the one who shapes it, saying, 'Stop, you're doing it wrong!' Does the pot exclaim, 'How clumsy can you be?'"

Isaiah 45:9 (NLT)

My thoughts turn back to my friend, Nate. While having been exposed to the truth of God for so many years, he never experienced the fullness of it. It was as if his ears were clogged and his eyes covered. Actually, it was just his natural default mode combined with the culture that convinced his conscience he was in control. Like all of us, Nate really believed that it was best if he shaped his own circumstances. The divine irony is that the circumstances he was attempting to control by avoiding, powering through, or merely coping, were the exact circumstances that God wanted to use to shape Nate into the likeness of Himself. Nate did not become open to this shaping until he came to the end of his reliance on himself. Only then would he let the Creator take over the molding of his clay (life).

The apostle Paul wanted the people of Corinth and us to understand that only after we turn toward the Lord will the true shaping of our lives begin:

> "But whenever anyone turns to the Lord, the veil is taken away... And we all, who with unveiled faces contemplate the Lord's glory, are being transformed into his image with ever-increasing glory, which comes from the Lord, who is the Spirit."

2 Corinthians 3:16-18

Am I saying that we are being shaped into gods? No. What I am saying is that God wants to transform us into His likeness so that we will reflect His image and draw others to Him. Instead of being gods, we are being called to be reflectors of God. I realize this idea does not bring about applause from the crowd and is not on the list of the best paying jobs. But when lived out in whatever context of God-given giftedness, be it as an employee, parent, student, or aging sage, you may actually receive admiration from your peers or inquiries into your secrets of success. If done with love and humility, God will get all the credit, for His character will shine through you.

Like all of us who get lost in our default mode, Nate had been attempting to reflect more and more of himself to the world. He had been attempting to shine himself into the eyes of many for self-glorification. Now, in his new life, Nate attempts to reflect God to the world, so that God's glory can be seen.

A different translation of the same verse from the apostle Paul conveys this idea well:

> "So all of us who have had that veil removed can see and reflect the glory of the Lord. And the Lord—who is the Spirit—makes us more and more like him as we are changed into his glorious image."

> **2 Corinthians 3:18 (NLT)**

God wants to use circumstances to shape us. The problem that most of us have with this lesson is that we struggle to believe that God would use pain, struggle, and discomfort as vehicles to reshape our flawed character. Furthermore, we simply don't like to believe we are flawed. But watch the news, read the newspaper, look at your family background, and then go ask your spouse, kids, or a close friend if they think you are flawed. For it is then that you will get an accurate picture of others and yourself.

Another problem is that it is tough to get our attention. Pain, struggle, and discomfort in various forms are the only things powerful enough to slow us down and humble us to the point of looking up to God for wisdom. Dallas Willard, the former Dean of Philosophy at the University of Southern California and the modern-day equivalent to C.S. Lewis writes, "It is only in the heart of pain and suffering, both mental and physical, that real human character is forged."[7]

When I look back on my life, I see that I learned the most about myself and God while in the midst of family alcoholism, failures in academics, lack of success in previous jobs, struggles in my ministry, aggravations in marriage and relationships, an unknown future, loss of dear peers, and the painful death of a child. Specifically, these seasons of life have acted as catalysts for me to take stock of my own character and purpose. During the seasons when I allowed God to hold me and mold me, the end result always seemed to be a new direction with renewed perspective and a more God-like character. In the times I tried to remain in control and left God out, the outcome included anxiety, endless striving, pride, or self-pity. Therapists and psychologists would recommend "letting go," "accepting our limitations," and/or "seeking a growth mindset." Spiritually, it is best described as "surrendering to God," "having grace for oneself," and "becoming more Christ-like."

Many ask the question, "Is God punishing me with these challenging circumstances?" Wayne Grudem, professor of biblical and systematic theology at Trinity Evangelical Divinity School, explains this concept so clearly:

"Sometimes suffering is simply a result of living in a sinful, fallen world and sometimes it is because God is disciplining us (for our good)... Not all discipline is in order to correct us from sins that we have committed; it can also be allowed by God (in the form of suffering) to strengthen us in order that we may gain greater ability to trust God and resist sin in the challenging path of obedience... Therefore, we should see all the hardship and suffering that comes to us in life as something that God brings to us to do us good, strengthening our trust in him and our obedience and ultimately increasing our ability to glorify him."[8]

Jesus' brother, James, stated something similar:

> "Consider it pure joy, my brothers and sisters, whenever you face trials of many kinds, because you know that the testing of your faith develops perseverance. Let perseverance finish its work so that you may be mature and complete, not lacking anything. If any of you lacks wisdom, you should ask God, who gives generously to all without finding fault, and it will be given to you. But when you ask, you must believe and not doubt, because the one who doubts is like a wave of the sea, blown and tossed by the wind."
>
> **James 1:2-6**

our next action step

As day turned to evening on Friday, September 7, 2001 just prior to 7:00 p.m., I realized the trial of a lifetime had descended upon us. Our most recent discussion with the doctors had forecast our next action step, which would be a breathing test for Emma around 8:00 p.m. As I walked out of the room to make some more phone calls to friends and family, I was relieved that we had made the decision to "wait and see." At that moment, the circumstances of the past that had shaped us to this point were not in my forethought, because the circumstances that lay ahead were making me feel like wobbly clay on the wheel. We obviously needed more help from the Potter.

reflection & challenges

How have you been shaped by past circumstances?

Currently, what circumstances is God using to shape you, and are you willing to let Him be your Potter?

How do you feel about pain being your greatest teacher?

Great is Thy faithfulness, O God my Father;
There is no shadow of turning with Thee,
Thou changest not, Thy compassions they fail not,
As Thou hast been, Thou forever wilt be.

Thomas O. Chisolm

LESSON SIX

let God in

A s emma's usual bedtime of 7:30 p.m. approached on Friday, September 7, 2001, she lay in the hospital with no brain activity and connected to a respirator. This was clearly not going to be a typical bedtime ritual for us. Bedtime was often the best time around our house. What is it about letting freshly bathed toddlers run around the house naked that makes everybody giggle? Putting on warm pajamas, brushing teeth, and reading books was so sweet when our kids would willingly participate and were not over-tired. Individually praying with each child was also part of our bedtime ritual, and while they were too young to understand intellectually, they would engage in the process if we made it fun.

Emma, in her cute, pink, big-flowered onesie jammies would always walk in her room when I told her it was time to get in her prayer chair. She would climb up into her just-above-ground-level, over-stuffed, multi-colored easy chair that her Nana had given her, then lay horizontally across it on her back, with her thumb in her mouth and blankie held tight. I would assume my position lying below her on the floor, reading the same two books to her every night. Next, I would tell her it was time to pray. She would get on the ground and kneel, facing the chair with her head in it as she mimicked the prayers I gave her. In the moment, I hoped I was teaching a child the beginning of being humble before the One who made her. With the completion of her "prayers," I would hold her and give her a verbal blessing, letting her know that God made her and loved her, that He had plans for her, and that He wanted to help her.

wishing for normalcy

With our day turning into a nightmare, all I wished for was for us to be back home, managing the typical witching hours with our three beauties from 5-8:00 p.m., rather than being trapped in the current disheartening descent of the evening. At 5:30 p.m., instead of prepping dinner and playing with kids, we faced hearing about Emma's brain condition and our options. At 6:00 p.m., instead of sitting down for dinner, we were begging God and wandering the hospital, seeking and finding answers from a teenager about our daughter's next survival steps. At 7:30 p.m., instead of baths, brushing teeth, books, prayers, and snuggling in bed, we were making calls all over the country to inform others and clarifying next steps with the doctors. Oh, how I yearned for the sweet mundane (often irritating) routine of home over this!

But by 8:00 p.m., the atrium lobby was overflowing with folks who had come to support us. Just a short time later, by 8:10 p.m., many had begun to pack into Emma's room for a breathing test, which involved turning the respirator off to see if she could breathe on her own.

The scene involved thirteen friends, two sets of in-laws, three doctors, a respiratory therapist, and Missy and me waiting to catch a glimpse of the breath of life from our little one. As we huddled in the darkened PICU corner room, lit only by monitors and a fluorescent light on the wall just beyond the head of Emma's bed, I panned the room and saw most couples holding each other, most eyes glazed with tears, and most verbalizing incomprehensible prayers. The emotion in the room brought forth a physical humidity and a spiritual anticipation that could be felt on our skin and in our souls. We were waiting on a miracle.

So with the declaration that the respirator was indeed off, all eyes fixated on either Emma's scarred chest or the white line on the breathing monitor, for either would indicate that Emma had life.

It did not go as hoped—no movement, no miracle. During those agonizing and endless minutes, we watched in silence for the breath of life—a twitch, a puff, a subtle rise of her chest, or a beep or signal from the monitor. But nothing ever happened. She just laid there in a motionless, lifeless, breathless state. After giving me a negative head shake from across the room, the doctor signaled to stop the test and then told the tech to reengage the respirator. Around 8:30 p.m., as the unwanted melody of the respirator began again, it seemed to create a deep rhythm of sadness and silence in the room. There was nothing to be said. The obvious had been stated by the inactivity seen.

Needing relief from what seemed inevitable, Missy and I left the room to have a brief discussion in the hallway. We quickly agreed again to "wait and see," but did not know what that looked like. All we knew was Missy deeply desired to just hold her daughter and I ached to know how this would end. Around 8:45 p.m., I gathered my Bible and told Missy that I was going to the third floor to be alone to sort through my thoughts and feelings with God. I asked my dad to come get me if needed.

desperate for an answer

As I came out of the elevator on the third floor, I began to search for a quiet place and was continually asking God this question in my head, "What do you want to happen?" I was desperate for an answer. The enclosed phone area provided the place I was looking for. It was out of the way of the main flow of the third floor and included a chair and table so I could journal. Once settled in, I dialed my sister, Karen, who lived in Boston.

The phone call to my sister was touching and tear-filled. Karen, my only sibling, though four years older, had always been an encouraging presence in my life. The scrapbook pictures of our youth reflected it. Karen holding me as a little baby and playing with me as a toddler, the two of us dressing up together as monsters during our elementary years, and her joyfully embracing me at my high school and college graduations. During the reality of life between the pictures, she protected and included me. When our mom and dad had arguments in the kitchen, she sat with me at the top of the stairs. When the nights were scary for me, she shared her blanket as I lay below her bed on the floor in her room. Whether in the neighborhood or at the house with her friends or on a drive to Dairy Queen as "Horton, her copilot" or during college visits, she always welcomed me. I often said that she was "my biggest fan for no good reason." For most of my life, I lived out the relationship on my selfish, younger brother terms. I got her to take me places, do and buy things for me, while only visiting or calling when it was convenient for me.

That changed for me after moving to California, with my faith coming alive and each of us getting married and having kids. Simply put, I realized how much her presence mattered in my life. It was a gift God had given me. I was a young boy who needed encouragement and I was blessed with a sister who had done just that. From that point forward, my phone calls and plans to connect became more deliberate and intentional. So in our current circumstances, her absence had a weight like no other. At this moment in life, I wasn't in need of her encouragement. I just desired her presence because we had shared so much life up to this point. Was my daughter really going to die without the presence of my sister and her husband, David (a.k.a. Bear)? Just a month prior, we had been all together at their place on a lake. It didn't seem right. We could barely get through our final words on the phone as the wave of tears interrupted. She said, "I am so sorry we cannot get there any sooner. I wish we could." My reply: "Me... too." After hanging up, I just sat and sobbed. Reality was sinking in. The end was coming, and I could foresee who was going to be present and who was not.

After wiping away my tears into the sleeves of my mustard-colored Oxford button-down shirt, I knew I needed to look into God's Word and journal my thoughts and prayers to Him to gain perspective. My mind had been racing in overdrive since the two nights prior, when Emma's seizures had begun. My head pounded from sobbing and from having not eaten since noon.

Even as a Christ follower of ten years, vocationally working as a pastor for almost six years, and holding a masters of divinity in the study of God, I was stumped about where to look in the Bible for the answers to our dilemma. Where does this historical text, written over 2000 years ago, specifically address the issue of life support and how to handle it? Bottom line, it doesn't. However, I had learned from past experiences that the ancient and inspired truth of the Bible bridges into the present if we are open to it. The Bible tells us that God designed Scripture as a way of communicating His ways to us on earth.

The following passages, which I had come to believe in, confirm this thought. First, the words of Jesus to His disciples ensure that the Holy Spirit that lives in us as believers will expose us to the actual knowledge of God:

"All that belongs to the Father is mine. That is why I said the Spirit will receive from me what he will make known to you."

John 16:15

Next, these words explain to the Jews that the words of Jesus, spoken and recorded in the Scriptures will convey the ways of God:

"In the past God spoke to our ancestors through the prophets at many times and in various ways, but in these last days he has spoken to us by his Son…"

Hebrews 1:1-2

Peter's words confirm that those who have written the Scriptures are inspired by the Holy Spirit so God's ways could be heard:

"Above all, you must realize that no prophecy in Scripture ever came from the prophet's own understanding, or from human initiative. No, those prophets were moved by the Holy Spirit, and they spoke from God."

2 Peter 1:20-21 (NLT)

The words from the apostle Paul to his protégé Timothy tell us about the viability of Scripture and its usefulness:

"All Scripture is God-breathed and is useful for teaching, rebuking, correcting and training in righteousness, so that the servant of God may be thoroughly equipped for every good work."

2 Timothy 3:16-17

The book of James and various other verses further support the concept that God wants to make His ways clear to us and is willing to help us understand if we will simply include Him during our time of need:

> "If any of you lacks wisdom, you should ask God, who gives generously to all without finding fault, and it will be given to you."
>
> **James 1:5**

> "Come near to God and he will come near to you..."
>
> **James 4:8**

> "Ask and it will be given to you; seek and you will find; knock and the door will be opened to you."
>
> **Matthew 7:7**

It was with this knowledge and the past experience of learning from Scripture in times of need that I opened my Bible to the book of Psalms. Why did I choose the Psalms? They had proven loyal in prior instances with Emma. Furthermore, King David wrote many of the Psalms. Throughout his life, he had found himself in many desperate situations, whether it was running from his enemies, heading to battle, or confessing his sinfulness. On this night, I, too, was desperate.

As I began flipping backwards through the Psalms, my eyes were drawn to the opening line of Psalm 130 resting near the top of the page. "Out of the depths I cry to you, O Lord." I read on, for it matched my emotions:

> "Lord, hear my voice. Let your ears be attentive to my cry for mercy. If you, LORD, kept a record of sins, Lord, who could stand? But with you there is forgiveness, so that we can, with reverence, serve you. I wait for the LORD, my whole being waits, and in his word I put my hope. I wait for

the Lord more than watchmen wait for the morning, more than watchmen wait for the morning. Israel, put your hope in the LORD, for with the LORD is unfailing love and with him is full redemption."

Psalm 130:2-7

While I did not know the extent of the literal situation about which the psalmist was writing, I could infer and later confirm that the author was in the midst of his own adversity, crying out for mercy. Like the psalmist, I was crying out for mercy, and I yearned for the Lord to be attentive to my pleas. I held on to the promise that God gives wisdom. Three times the desperate author says he will wait for the Lord. I took this as a sign from God that I, too, was to somehow be patient and wait. But for how long? Graciously, the answer was made clear in the next line. I was to be more patient than the all-night watchmen guarding the city, who were waiting for the morning sunrise so they could be released from duty.

I read the passage a second time and thought to myself, "What time is sunrise, and is this the time to release Emma?" I had remembered the doctors saying that twelve hours after being pronounced brain dead, a patient on a respirator would have to be checked to see if they could breathe on their own. Twelve hours from the 5:30 p.m. diagnosis was an obvious 5:30 a.m. Inwardly, my default mode was telling me I was reading too much into Scripture and that I was attaching significance to unrelated events in history. Yet, I knew Scripture had spoken to me like this before.

In an attempt to gain clarity, I journaled a prayer to God on the blank pages in the back of my Bible. I began by putting the date and time:

9/7/2001
9:51 p.m.

Lord,

I praise you for the day. You have given us Emma's life and it is you who takes it away. Thank you for what you have taught me and given me through her. Lord I want to wait, but should I release her? I want to let you work fully. Is there a correct thing to do?

What do you mean for me and our circumstances from Psalm 130:5-6, "I wait for the Lord, my soul waits, and in his word I put my hope. My soul waits for the Lord more than watchmen wait for the morning, more than watchmen wait for the morning."

Thank you for Jesus, my salvation, your grace, Missy, Sadie, Emma, Elise, my family and friends and life's circumstances.

Give me wisdom,
Brian H. Rhen

lesson confirmed

My dad arrived about halfway through my tearful journaling to inform me it had been just over an hour. I asked him to tell Missy that I would be down shortly. Earlier in the hour, he had brought me food while I was in the midst of the phone conversation with my sister. His support typified the consistent role he had played as a providing father throughout my life. He had never done it with much fanfare, words, or physical touch, but had always showed love and support by meeting physical needs and by being present.

After finishing my journaling, I sat quietly. The answer seemed obvious through the repetition of the verses. The passage was about crying out to God in the midst of need, letting Him in fully, and having the patience to wait and see what God would do. I still did not have a biblical answer to releasing someone off life support. But I had my next step— "wait for the morning."

I found Missy back in the room in a rocking chair with Emma cradled in her arms. She was stroking her hair. The sight was surreal. In some ways, it looked like any other night when she was rocking her to sleep like she so often did. However, the hospital gown and all the tubes brought reality back very quickly. I was in shock and could not cry; rather, I was consumed with telling Missy what I felt God had spoken to me upstairs. She went along with my interpretation. I was not convinced she believed it, but it was the more hopeful option. I suggested we bring everyone into the room for a time of prayer and anointing with oil. My rationale was based on obedience and faith. I knew the Bible instructed to anoint the sick, and I was hopeful for a miracle. Furthermore, I wanted to give God the opportunity to move in any way He wanted, whether it was healing her in a miraculous way or guiding us.

My logic overshadowed my faith as folks entered her room, yet I knew others among us believed in the miraculous. From 10:30 to 11:30 p.m., more than twenty people crowded back into Emma's room. I sat next to Missy in the rocking chair and watched as others filed in, taking seats on the floor, standing along the wall, or sitting on Emma's empty bed that had been pushed aside. I told them what God's Word had revealed and what had happened with Francisco. I asked them if they would join in by reading Scripture out loud, praying out to God, and anointing her with oil in the hope of the miraculous. For some, this was a common ritual; for others, it was most likely unique and a bit uneasy and unknown.

For the next hour, we welcomed God's presence in the room, sang songs, shared stories, anointed Emma with oil, and read Scripture aloud. Not all participated verbally, but all were engaged emotionally. It was wonderful to share our intimacy with God with those of our family and friends who had never had such an experience. My emotions exploded in uncontrolled sobbing like many others after my colleague and friend, Gary, anointed Emma with oil and began to recite from Mark 5:35-43 (NLT):

> "While he was still speaking to her, messengers arrived from the home of Jairus, the leader of the synagogue. They told him, 'Your daughter is dead. There's no use troubling the Teacher now.' But Jesus overheard them and said to Jairus, 'Don't be afraid. Just have faith.' Then Jesus stopped the crowd and wouldn't let anyone go with him except Peter, James, and John. When they came to the home of the synagogue leader, Jesus saw much commotion and weeping and wailing. He went inside and asked, 'Why all this commotion and weeping? The child isn't dead; she's only asleep.' The crowd laughed at him. But he made them all leave, and he took the girl's father and mother and his three disciples into the room where the girl was lying. Holding her hand, he said to her, 'Talitha koum,' which means 'Little girl, get up!' And the girl, who was twelve years old, immediately stood up and walked around! They were overwhelmed and totally amazed."

I sobbed, for I knew I had the limited faith of the messengers. Yet an ounce of me expected her to move as Gary repeated over and over again, "Get up little girl! Get up!" I knew Gary. I knew, like Tony, he believed it could happen. I repeated the same words, "Get up little girl. Get up little girl…" over and over again in a whispery tone as I cried. She never moved. I knew God had heard, yet I believed it was not His will for her.

My mind flashed back to some five hours earlier, to the hallway just outside the CAT scan lab where Emma had been tested. During that time, I had left Missy in the conference room and was pacing the hallway, talking to God. As I walked to the end of the hallway, I looked to the left and the right down the long narrow corridor and was shocked by its emptiness and stillness. Previously, these corridors had been bustling with hospital traffic. As I stood there, I asked God to give me a sign if Emma was gone. The area remained vacant and motionless for what seemed like minutes before an Indian doctor entered the space at the far right end, breaking the stillness. I believed the stillness was the sign—she was gone at that point.

Remembering that flashback gave me peace in an odd sort of way. The stillness of Emma in the midst of clamoring prayer paralleled the silence in that hallway in the midst of the chaotic hospital. Neither satisfied me, but I believed God knew what He was doing.

By 11:30 p.m., we ended our formal prayer time and put in a home video of our kids in the VCR in the room. The mood in the room changed from somber to reflective and joyous in pockets, as people chatted, embraced, and watched the video. Near midnight, Missy requested to have Emma lay on the bed with her so she could cuddle and get some sleep. I informed folks that it was time to say goodbye. The mood changed back to somber as folks walked over to us, one by one, with Missy holding Emma in the rocking chair, to say goodbye. At the time, nobody knew there would be another goodbye chance in the morning. With their departure, it seemed like the end had already occurred. Missy laid down with Emma on the bed, and I pulled up a chair and a blanket and recommitted to watching the video running in the backdrop.

At 1:30 a.m., I walked out to find my parents and, to my surprise, found all but a few of the family and friends still at the hospital. As I toured the second floor, the place looked like a living morgue of our friends spread out wherever they could find comfortable space. Someone had borrowed a bunch of white bedsheets, and everyone was using them to stay warm and keep the fluorescent light out so they could sleep. Back in the room, I dozed on and off as my eyes went from the rolling video to the bed where my wife and daughter lay. Around 4:30 a.m., I became obsessed with figuring out the time of sunrise, as that represented morning and our next deadline. I headed down to the first-floor lobby to see if I could find a freshly delivered paper. Fortunately, I found one. The *Palo Alto Daily* stated that sunrise was scheduled for 6:45 a.m. My stomach began to feel like it did in college when I pulled an all-nighter for an early morning exam and knew I was not ready. So, I went back to the room to sit and wait.

prayer answered

I watched the clock between intervals of dozing and hated every minute of the 5:00 a.m. hour, for it brought me closer to the morning. Just after 6:00 a.m., both sets of our parents surprisingly filed in. I was a bit shocked and angered when someone asked me, "What have you decided?" I didn't have an answer.

In an unconscious attempt to escape, I told our parents that we would wait for our doctors who had not yet arrived and that I needed to make phone calls to dear friends back East. After making my first phone call and sharing our situation with my college roommate, John, I came back in to have a discussion with Missy.

In our short conversation, I asked her what she thought we should do. Her reply was to wait indefinitely. I was shocked by her answer, which was now opposite of mine. Over the previous twelve hours, God had touched us and changed both of our minds, yet we lacked unity. We decided that I would make my other phone call, then we would have a few friends come have a discussion with us about what the Bible says about releasing one from life support. Before making the phone call, I went out to find the "few friends" and to my surprise, all of our friends were now sitting together in one specific area of the second floor. Since I could not invite only a few people in front of everyone, I went back to Missy and told her that God obviously wanted this to be an open theological discussion in the atrium lounge area.

After calling my childhood friend, Keith, I found Missy sitting with our friends. The group was silent with their heads down, looking at their Bibles. The only thing that could be heard was the flipping of pages. I asked Missy what she'd said to them. She told me she informed everyone that we were looking for the biblical view on releasing someone from life support and wanted only specific biblical passages quoted and not personal opinion. In frustration, I said, "People are going to have to give us their opinions, for the Bible is not clear on it." I was not looking forward to this debate about Emma's future being played out amongst so many. I felt there was no way this was going to help us come to a concrete decision. However, the miraculous happened.

Within a few minutes, the rustling of pages was broken up by the voice of my supervisor and senior pastor, Jon, who had walked across the open area and sat on the floor below us. He asked us a series of questions about where we were with the situation. We conveyed how our views had switched during the night, yet we still did not have unity. At that point, he then asked the others to begin sharing their findings. Some of our friends took turns sharing verses, while others admitted they were as confused as we were. In all, we were given seven passages, but it was the second one, given by Missy, that united us.

> "Then the LORD God formed the man from the dust of the
> ground. He breathed the breath of life into the man's nostrils,
> and the man became a living person."
>
> **Genesis 2:7 (NLT)**

I said to Missy, "God has taken the breath of life from Emma, so it is okay to release her if she cannot breathe on her own." Nodding her head in an affirming manner, she agreed without hesitation. We both decided to run the breathing test one more time, to see if the breath of life was present, and if not, we would release her.

the end is near

Ironically, I thought the process of discussing the life support issue would take an hour or more. Yet, in less than five minutes, God united us as a couple and as a community of believers through His Word. To me, this was a miracle! The morning had brought forth the final step in our process and the answer we had been instructed to wait for throughout the night. Desperation had led to letting Him in, and that changed everything. As we closed our Bibles, we paused to pray together—giving thanks to God and everyone there. Then Missy and I stood up and headed back towards Emma's room.

reflection & challenges

What desperate circumstances have you let God into or wish you had?

What holds you back from letting Him in?

What might be the most natural way God speaks to you? (i.e. prayer, His Word, others, dreams, song, circumstances, etc.)

You have created us for yourself
and our hearts are restless
until they rest in you.

St. Augustine

LESSON SEVEN

life finds meaning in death

'VE HEARD IT SAID that death and beauty are the greatest catalysts for us to grow in our understanding of God and life. I found this to be true as I entered Emma's room for the last time just after 7:40 a.m. on September 8, 2001. Emma lay there on the bed connected to so many monitors, machines, and other medical contraptions, but disconnected from how much she was helping us understand the meaning of life. The ironic fact is that she never knew the meaning of life. And actually, many people never even ponder the meaning of life, for it seems an unsolvable mystery.

As a mere toddler, I believe Emma was living out the meaning of life more than many adults. To love God, to love others, and to use our God-given abilities to bring Him glory in whatever context we are placed is what I hold to as the meaning of life. This is based on my understanding of the words God and Jesus recorded in the Bible, along with the testimonies of those who followed them. As for Emma, her simple understanding of God was growing, her love for others was obvious, and she brought Him glory in her play and in the sweetness of her connection with others. Culture, intelligence, and her own default mode had not yet derailed her. For most adults, including myself, it takes trial and error, pain, tragedy, or death to teach us the true meaning of life. God was graciously using Emma as our young little guide into these depths.

the final test

Prior to the final breathing test, we told the doctors that if Emma failed it, we would immediately release her from the respirator. In the room on that early September morning, were several doctors, a few nurses, our parents, and two close friends. Missy asked for a passage from the Bible to be read prior to starting the test, for it represented how God had shown us His great mercy by providing direction in our unique situation. One of our friends read aloud:

> "Because of the LORD's great love we are not consumed,
> for his compassions never fail. They are new every morning;
> great is your faithfulness. I say to myself, 'The LORD is my
> portion; therefore I will wait for him.' The LORD is good
> to those whose hope is in him, to the one who seeks him…"

Lamentations 3:22-25

After it was read, we prayed for God's will to be done. We both assumed she would not breathe. Over the previous twelve hours, the movements of God seemed to make it obvious that we would be releasing her in minutes. The questions in our minds were very practical. How long would she last once off the respirator? Who should be in the room as she dies? The doctors answered the first question. They told us it could be up to five to ten minutes. We never discussed the second question. For the moment, the right people seemed to be in the room. Everyone else that was still out in the hospital lobby had already gotten to say their goodbyes around midnight.

Again, the breathing test lasted less than ten minutes. Emma's chest never moved, indicating that the breath of life was gone from her. The doctors asked us if Missy would like to hold her once she was disconnected from the respirator and other monitors. Emma would be able to die in the arms of her mother. We agreed, and the nurses and doctors in the room began to maneuver to make this happen.

It was then that I watched as death and beauty collided over the next hour. After taking out Emma's breathing tube and disconnecting her from all monitors, she was placed into Missy's arms. I sat down next to them. Emma, with her typical bluish color and matted blonde hair, clothed in a small hospital gown, looked like she was sleeping. All eyes were on mother and child, with a window backdrop of a low rising sun, dominated by a hazy gray-blue sky. It was a few minutes after 8:00 a.m. Missy broke the silence and asked, "How will we know when her heart has stopped?" As the doctor came close, checking Emma's pulse, he replied somberly, "It has. Her heart has stopped, I am sorry." I lifted up my head and proclaimed gently to all, "She is dead. Her heart has stopped." It had taken less than a minute.

a beautiful death

Around 8:05 a.m. on Saturday, September 8, 2001, our daughter, Emma Grace Rhen, died and went to heaven at the age of two years and just shy of four months. Typically, on a Saturday like this one, I would have been on my way to Safeway with Sadie and Emma in the baby jogger, along with Baxter, our dog, in tow on his leash. Missy would have been feeding Elise or attempting to get more sleep if Elise complied. No extended family, no friends, no thoughts of heaven, just bagels and donuts and silly conversations with two little girls still in their jammies. At Safeway, our biggest decision of the morning would have been whether to get Baxter a blueberry or plain bagel. He liked either.

Regardless of where I usually was or wanted to be, I knew I was meant to be in that hospital room on that day. The unspoken voice of God through my reading in the book of Job at the kitchen table on that late Saturday night, back on May 22, 1999, had forecast her impending death to me. Plus, the divine unfolding of events since arriving at the hospital and the journey of the previous two years enabled me to not be surprised. However, was I in shock? Sure. Was I overwhelmed with tears of a deep, deep sadness? Completely. Yet, there was something peacefully beautiful happening around Emma's death, which I was able to witness.

Upon looking up in the midst of my sorrow, what I saw in that hospital room was raw, uncontrollable brokenness. Grown men were shaking with emotion like I had never seen before. People were sobbing and holding one another. Kleenex, handkerchiefs, bare hands, and shirtsleeves were being used to combat the endless flow of tears. Few distinguishable words were spoken. Only gasps for air could be heard between the cries and the sniffling. Then, without command, each person in the room came and knelt in front of Missy, Emma, and me. Some touched Emma, some hugged us, some did nothing, but all said their final goodbye. It was a repeat of the scene from the evening before, but even more beautiful.

To my surprise, those waiting in the open lounge area began to trickle in one by one or two by two as part of the final farewell procession. Soon the room was bursting with a fresh lament of tears of those who had weathered the night or who had come back for the morning. They had been a part of the journey and longed to see it through to completion. It was a needed ending to a tragic time spent together. Faces of friends who had neither visited nor been with us through the night surprisingly entered. My tears became fueled with gratefulness for their concern and efforts to join us. I attempted to greet each person with eye contact and a nod after they had all taken their initial look at Emma and Missy.

I can honestly say that I enjoyed this extended time with all. It was so rich and so, so painful, yet oddly wordless and deeply satisfying. We were in the presence of God and among those who loved us. It was a such a sweet, tragic, communal moment. As they departed, I yearned for them to linger. My only regret is that my sister, Karen, and the rest of my brothers- and sisters-in-law were unable to share in this terribly wonderful moment.

Prior to filling out final paperwork, they placed Emma back on her bed and gave Missy the opportunity to clean her. Her color was changing to a deeper blue, but she otherwise looked asleep. Her short, wavy blonde hair was still matted to her head, and it had a yellow tint to it instead of its usual white sheen. As we stood there, not wanting or knowing how to leave, Emma's surgeon entered the room, and we gladly received him. He apologized again with tears in his eyes for this unexpected outcome. The conversation bounced from encouraging him to discussing his daughter of a similar age. Death had us speaking directly from the heart.

As we walked out of the PICU doors into the atrium hallway, we were greeted by teary-eyed faces of a few more friends who had just arrived to support us. I was disappointed that they did not get to see Emma and fully experience what God had done, but at that point, there was no turning back time.

Around 10:00 a.m., we headed to meet our parents for breakfast at a local restaurant. How could we be hungry at a time like this? We were not, but anything was a better option than going home and telling almost-four-year-old Sadie that her sister was not coming home.

reality strikes

On the way to the restaurant, we called Missy's brother, Peter, from my cell phone. We thought we should have him update the website that had helped others stay connected to the situation. It seemed ridiculous, outright harsh, and too shocking to leave a message on a website saying your daughter has just died, yet, we knew it was the fastest and easiest way to communicate it. He posted the following message:

Saturday, September 8, 8:05 a.m.

It gives us great sadness and joy to report that Emma Grace Rhen passed away and went to heaven. Emma's passing was caused by extensive brain swelling and complications from the surgery.

The restaurant was packed, and nobody in the place had any knowledge of our present situation, so it was good to be there with our parents. Though we were still in shock, we found pockets of normalcy in our typical family conversations about great food from other places, fabulous deals on things, and the various goings-on with other family members. But in between the typical bits of small talk were the reflections and tears about Emma, her dying process, the staff at Stanford, and the community of support. We were there for just over an hour. However, the longer we stayed, the more irritated I became with the dual reality we were living in. I wanted to stand up at one point and yell to everyone in the room who was feasting prior to a Saturday kickoff and dressed mostly in Stanford cardinal red, "Does anybody realize that my child has just died?"

We drove home with our meals in our throats. We had made this drive from the hospital so many times over the previous two-plus years. Heading home from an appointment or from a visit with Emma after surgery had always been a positive experience. But not this final journey. Moving forward, we would have no reason to return to the hospital. Sadie and Elise's pediatrician was located elsewhere, and all of Emma's doctors at the hospital no longer needed to meet with us. It seemed so abruptly final, odd, and unfair. Our discussion in the car focused on how we were going to tell Sadie. We decided to avoid it until we called our friend, Sue, my colleague and a fantastic therapist.

Once home, we stalled Sadie by telling her that Emma was still at the hospital. It wasn't technically a lie, but it sure felt like one. After feeding Sadie, putting her down for a nap, and handing Elise off to a grandparent, Missy suggested that the two of us get some sleep. I took a shower to get the hospital grime off and to change out of the clothes I had worn for over twenty-four hours. The irony was that I was wearing the same shirt I had worn the morning of the initial diagnosis some two years earlier. God's timing or my limited wardrobe—who knows? In the sanctuary of the shower, my tears were washed away as soon as they surfaced, but nothing could penetrate and alleviate the ache in my soul.

As I was getting into bed, I remembered that I had not spoken to my buddy, Erin, who had recently moved to LA. I caught him on his cell phone in the middle of a huge recreation field, where he was running a sports outreach event for his church. I apologized for not calling him earlier and told him Emma had died earlier that morning. He was the first person outside of the hospital that I declared our reality to. I thought I would not have tears left to cry, but mine freshly flowed with his. Our conversation was brief; it closed with each of us telling the other we loved each other. Death brings those who are meaningful to your mind.

Waking up from my nap was the worst. It stung. I did not want to leave the room. Dealing with people seemed pointless. However, being close to dinner, I was hungry and eager to see my sister and family who were arriving from Boston. The distraction of cousins would be good for Sadie. Our friends, the Johnsons, "popped-in" to say they were thinking of us. With more family arriving, it seemed like a holiday. My head pounded from the noisy toddlers, and everything I ate tasted bland. My spirit was worn, my hope was lost, and I had great anxiety over telling Sadie that her sister had gone to heaven. What if it made her hate God? What if it gave her a scarring view of Jesus? What if losing her sister broke her cheerful spirit forever?

It was near bedtime when we told her. The irony was that we took her into Emma's room and had her sit in the "prayer chair." Missy had spoken to Sue, who had helped us with what to say and what not to say. I began and Missy finished. Missy's last words were, "Emma is in heaven and won't be coming home." In shock, I watched Sadie absorb the information and simultaneously cry out as she threw herself on the floor, "No! I want my sister!" Her response was so adult-like that it frightened me. She had gotten it. Nothing more needed to be explained. She rolled up in a ball on the floor, crying, and piercingly stated, "I want us to go to heaven as a family right now!" At that moment, she was speaking our hearts' desire. Since heaven wasn't an option, she moved all her clothes into Emma's room and climbed into Emma's crib to sleep for the next week.

fog rolls in

In time, Sadie's resilience was remarkable. I attribute it to her age, prayer, and the grace of God. We did not fare the same as Sadie. Life became foggy for both of us. Missy wanted to sleep a lot and I wanted to stay up a lot. Our therapist friend was so helpful, yet nothing could clear the fog. Even if it wasn't there in the morning when we woke up, it rolled in by the mid-afternoon and was always present in the evening. Under the "grief fog," we found ourselves on an unpredictable roller coaster ride that brought denial, anger, questioning, deep depression, and small moments of acceptance. But it also left us forgetful, irritable, irrational, and downright angry and ugly. The littlest things would enrage me, and I would find myself cursing, as I had prior to my rebirth in Christ. Questions of what we should and shouldn't have done with Emma's care haunted us. Little things, like unloading the dishwasher, became overwhelming. Lethargic was our common speed. When the fog rolled in thick, lying in bed and sobbing was our nightly ritual. Such loss; so painful; it weighed us down daily like a cold, wet blanket.

death brings perspective to life

Though we were suffering deeply, Emma's death was beginning to slowly birth a new perspective on life. In the small moments of acceptance, I felt blessed to have had such a tragic loss in my life because it was changing the way I lived, and I believe it was for the better. I often said the same thing regarding experiencing alcoholism in my immediate family and other challenges in my life. These experiences, if we allow them to shape us, result in questioning and pondering what really matters on earth and what the meaning of life is.

Death is one of the few things that really can bring perspective to life. It takes a lot for us to approach life differently. It is usually pain-causing tragedy that awakens us out of the comatose walk through life our default mode provides. I remember trying to get back into my regular workout routine about two weeks after Emma died. My default mode was telling me to get back on the horse and everything would be all right. So, on a sunny Saturday, I sat on the front porch, tied my running shoes, stretched a little, and took off to run my normal route. My legs felt like someone had injected cement into my veins. My breathing was awkward. Halfway through my familiar route, I stopped and asked myself, "Why am I running?" I could not answer the question. I walked home.

For the next few months in the fall of 2001, I walked a new route once a week. While leaving Sadie, almost four, at home with Missy, I'd push my growing six-month-old, Elise, in the baby jogger at a pace that only required flip-flops. After nap time, in the late afternoon on Saturdays, we'd stroll through our neighborhood, arriving at a local Catholic church. Dark and unlit, we would enter. With enough graham crackers to keep Elise busy for about a half hour, I would sit in a pew, pondering, crying, and praying. Once she got fussy, I'd hold her and walk throughout the church to get another twenty minutes. My new workout routine would end around ten minutes to five as parishioners began to enter for evening mass. I often came back to that church alone to find that same solace in the candles of the prayer room or in the enormous stained glass windows of the sanctuary. In those brief moments, sitting in His presence alleviated the sting of death within my soul.

glimmers of acceptance and new meaning

Although the grief fog was heavy during the initial months, we felt a slight clearing for the first time in early 2002. While relaxing alone without our kids in a hotel room in San Francisco on a chilly, foggy morning in mid-February, I read to Missy how God was bringing us through the pain of loss and longing.

> "…so after you have suffered a little while, he will restore, support, and strengthen you, and he will place you on a firm foundation."

> **1 Peter 5:10 (NLT)**

It had been only five months, but we had begun to experience the grace of God in our suffering. He was restoring our day-to-day joy for life a bit at a time, and our intense longings for little Emma were sadly lessening. Don't get me wrong, I am not saying we didn't miss her. Oh, we did—day and night. But the intensity was less. Ironically, the mundaneness of caring for two children under the age of five was not allowing us to focus our energy in that direction as often. Parenting was pulling us along. Meanwhile, the convictions about His goodness, the power of community, and the hope of heaven were being established within us. And we found He was giving us strength to begin to peel off the wet, cold, and heavy layers of grief that blanketed us. It may sound like God in some way came in and retrofitted our souls, similar to the way engineers strengthen a building after an earthquake. However, I would say He was in the process of rebuilding us completely from the ground up, for our souls had been demolished in her death.

The words of Solomon reflected what we had been through, were experiencing, and headed toward:

> "There is a time for everything, and a season for every activity
> under the heavens:
> a time to be born and a time to die,
> a time to plant and a time to uproot,
> a time to kill and a time to heal,
> a time to tear down and a time to build,
> a time to weep and a time to laugh,
> a time to mourn and a time to dance…"
>
> **Ecclesiastes 3:1-4**

reflection & challenges

What is the meaning of life to you?

How has death brought perspective to your life?

How have you grieved well (or not) after transition and tragedy?

Experience shared is wisdom and comfort
to the next participant.

Unknown

LESSON EIGHT

let your suffering be recycled

I T WAS WAY TOO CLOSE TO 2:00 P.M. on a Saturday in late March 2002. I was beginning to panic as I u-turned for the second time on Clinton Street in Redwood City, California. I was attempting to locate the memorial service I was supposed to preside over. I could feel the sweat dripping down my back into my shirt, which was tucked into my suit pants. As I looked at the clock, I internalized that if I didn't find it within about five minutes, it was going to get pretty humiliating.

The memorial service was for Brianna Marie—known as Bri, she was just a few months shy of nine years old when the breath of life was taken from her. Damage to her brain stem was the cause, which had been brought on by an attached tumor that had been surgically removed two years prior. Since her surgery, life had become very challenging medically, physically, and emotionally, yet her incredible perseverance and support of her family enabled her to attend camp in the summer of 2001 and third grade in the fall. By January 2002, the damaged brain stem knocked her unconscious and sent her to stay for good at Stanford's Lucile Packard Children's Hospital. Though she regained consciousness, her breathing required a respirator. Destined to never breathe on her own, her family had to come to terms with releasing her. On February 17, breathing assistance was removed. After overcoming seizures, she breathed on her own until the 21st, which was her eight-and-three-quarters birthday. Her breathing ceased just after the school bell rang at 2:23 p.m., her favorite numbers. Bri was cremated with her teddy bear and homework folder.

Her mom, Catherine, through a friend, had heard about me, a local pastor who had recently lost a young child. So began numerous conversations between Catherine, her ex-husband, Mark, and myself. As a child, Mark had been connected to our church through his mom, and he now lived in Sacramento. Our first connection was over the phone, and I could hear the sound of grief in his voice. In his descriptions of his current days, I knew he was in the same daily fog I had come through months earlier. I told him about some books that had been beneficial to me and promised to connect him with some local counselors in his area. Though I was playing the role of pastor, the conversation was surprisingly soothing to me, a grieving father. I hung up the phone and sat and looked out my window and sobbed. My tears consisted of compassion for him, the pain of my heart, and a cry for a different way for us both.

Catherine came to my office a few days after my conversation with Mark. Though we were different in gender, age, faith, and family backgrounds, our bond was built on the common experience of losing a child. Same hospital, similar life support issues, just a few months apart. We shared pictures, then our hearts. Sweet Bri had bright blue eyes and a smile so wide. As Catherine shared her story, my heart ached for her loss. Her experience as a nurse brought back terms and vivid visions of our hospital experience. The moment she departed and my office door closed, it began all over again. Hearing the details of her daughter's awareness that her own days were numbered and imagining the long sleepless nights with Bri's medication-induced sleep apnea, I found myself bent over in my chair, gasping for breath as the flood of emotion poured out of me. In the prior six months, no one had come into my office with a story that could reach so deeply into me. It was like my soul was being dredged—stirring up the debris of common pain, resulting in waves of tears on the surface.

Their story seemed much harder than ours. Emma never knew of her condition, nor gained enough consciousness to know the end was ever near, plus our nights were not sleepless. But Bri's story included all these things and more, including an eleven-year-old sister that was having extreme difficulty accepting the loss of her younger sibling.

I was glad we were focused on the goal of planning Bri's memorial service because it gave us a reason for a second meeting. There, I learned much more about Bri and Catherine's life journey and she learned of mine and Emma's. Through the exchange of stories and tears, I received my first glimpse into how God was recycling my suffering for the good of others and myself.

lost, but found

I remembered Catherine saying that balloons would be outside the women's club where the memorial was being held. It was so good to see those balloons as I drove in a rapid panic down Clinton Street on that sunny Saturday. While searching for a parking spot, my default mode had me questioning my ability to minister to this family. "I will be half the age of most of the people in this place... Why would they listen to me?... This is only my third memorial as a pastor. Shouldn't some fifty-five-year-old man or woman with about thirty of these under their belt be doing this?" My mind raged on until I gathered my Bible from the back of the car and began to walk toward the women's club. Desperate, I started a simple prayer-filled conversation out loud with God as I walked. "God, You know what You are doing; just use me how You want. You have given me my experience with Emma for this time—recycle my suffering for some good."

My prayer ended as I extended my hand and looked into Mark's eyes for the first time in person. For a few moments, he explained what he was going to share, and I told him it would be perfect. Though I still felt out of place, I mingled around and introduced myself to a few folks. By the time things were about to begin, I felt led that God had brought me there to share our story to begin to bring healing to theirs. As I stepped up to the podium, I disregarded my prepared notes, introduced myself, and began sharing from my heart.

lesson confirmed

About five years earlier, I had read a book by Henri Nouwen, entitled *The Wounded Healer.* I was struck by the way he thought understanding one's suffering was essential to helping others who also suffer. He writes,

"For a deep understanding of his own pain makes it possible for him to convert his weakness into strength and to offer his own experience as a source of healing to those who are often lost in the darkness of their own misunderstood suffering."9

He goes on to explain the role of one who ministers:

"Perhaps the main task of the minister is to prevent people from suffering for the wrong reasons. Many people suffer because of the false suppositions on which they have based their lives. That supposition is that there should be no fear or loneliness (or pain of any sort), no confusion or doubt… No minister can save anyone. He can only offer himself/herself as a guide to fearful people."[10]

Nouwen's description of a minister is not typical. This individual, he tells us, is not called to give quick, token answers to the problems of the day. Instead, a minister's role is to acknowledge and lament the reality of life's troubles, while pointing people in the right direction of proper wisdom and relief.

The Bible tells us that we are all called into ministry (2 Corinthians 3:6, 1 Peter 2:5,9). This is possible, not because of our uniforms or degrees, but because of our stories and how we are all inextricably linked with God. He is the One who has created us. He loves us. He has pre-ordained plans for us. He wants to help us and He yearns for us to overcome our false suppositions and come to a full understanding of the knowledge of Him. Furthermore, God yearns for us to tell our stories (good and bad) in the context of our relationship with Him, so that others will find peace in the midst of their suffering and false assumptions.

> "All praise to the God, the Father of our Lord Jesus Christ. God is our merciful Father and the source of all comfort. He comforts us in all our troubles so that we can comfort others. When they are troubled, we will be able to give them the same comfort God has given us."

2 Corinthians 1:3-4 (NLT)

This passage details the heart of God. He is the One who is the source of comfort in all circumstances. Nothing can comfort like God the Father, for He is constant, loving, and ever present. Though men and women can be inconsistent, consumed with themselves and absent, in His mercy, God uses them as ointment and bandages on the wounds of the brokenhearted. In our scenarios of suffering, once touched by the comfort of God, we are able to pass it on to others. Ever since that

Saturday prayer, I have thought of this process as recycled suffering. God wastes no parts of the journey—especially the painful pieces. He wants us to experience His comfort in our suffering so that it can be recycled in the lives of others. Often, I envision this as a warm blanket from God, given to one in need. Initially, this blanket acts as a source of comfort for the one weathering the suffering. Then, once restored, that same blanket is passed on to another to comfort them.

The book of Corinthians goes on to teach us that we all are called to be ministers of reconciliation (2 Corinthians 5:18-19). A minister of reconciliation helps others restore their broken relationship with God. If we extend this definition, one who is unreconciled is suffering and needs to exchange their own false suppositions in their current situation or viewpoint with a renewed understanding. As followers of Christ, we are called to be ministers, guiding folks from the fears they are suffering and pointing them to where peace can be found in Him.

Sharing Scars

The process of recycling suffering requires gentleness on the part of the one with the scars of healing and openness on the part of the one with fresh wounds of suffering. In both cases, vulnerability and honesty are essential. Over the years, I have been on both sides of this dynamic, and it is incredible to see how God brings together the right people at the right time whenever healing or reconciliation is needed. Even more incredible is how God uses scars of any type, of a similar nature or not, to bond people together and begin the process that enables people to eventually come to terms with their suffering.

I have come to liken this process of sharing scars to how we did it as kids. The snapshot in my head is one of a boy pulling up his pant leg or hiking up his shirt just high enough to reveal a healing scar. The boy goes on to tell of the drama, and the one listening takes it in and uses it for their present or future experience of suffering.

During our deepest grief, many shared their scars with us. Letters, cards, phone calls, emails, or replies from Emma's website flowed in with similar lines like, "I thought this would help you." Whether they were stories of stillborn sons and daughters, their own prayers of comfort after losing a loved one, or reminders of who God is, they all acted as ointment on our fresh wounds. One day in January, a friend boldly and humbly sat down and let me know how not to handle my grief. Years prior, the grief of losing his child, along with his lack of self-control, sent him into a tailspin of activity that still haunts him and his marriage to this day. What a strong warning it was for me and such a vulnerable expression of recycled suffering.

God has also used different scars from the same people in our lives. A card about Emma's situation from a family friend, whose scars from alcoholism helped walk our family through the same issue some years earlier, reminded us about God's character. They wrote:

> "Oh—it is so hard to describe the sadness we feel for you.
> Although we cannot understand God's methods in dealing with
> life and death, we do know that we live in a box of space and time
> and cannot see spacelessness or eternity. But God is not within
> the shell of time and space. God is timeless and spaceless."

This family friend was sharing wisdom from their scars of loss, based on the passing of their twenty-one-year-old daughter in a car accident years prior.

When necessary, God uses even those with fresh wounds to act as comfort. Almost everyone seems to know someone or someone who knew someone killed in the senseless terrorist act of 9/11. As the World Trade Towers fell, my parents' dear neighborhood friends watched their worst fears come true. Sally and Bob Murphy lost their son, Kevin, in the attack on New York City, three days after Emma died. Kevin left behind a family with young kids like so many others. My parents were already with us on that tragic day because Emma's memorial was the next day. However, upon their return home, they formed a unique bond with the Murphys. The two sets of parents shared common blankets of comfort as they processed their respective losses in an eight-week grief group at their local Catholic church, which I believe was divinely inspired by a loving God.

the churning of recycled suffering

As time has gone by, I am amazed how God has used Emma's story and other stories to touch and connect folks in ways only He planned. Emma's memorial service was planned for September 12, 2001. On the morning of September 11, I was up prior to 7:00 a.m. PST with our six-month-old, Elise, when the phone rang. On the other end in a panic was my Aunt Pinky, calling from the Cleveland airport, informing me that New York City had been attacked and that she and her family could not fly out for the memorial service. She was crying, and all I could think of was that she had lost her mind. Within minutes after turning on the TV, I watched the first of two World Trade Towers fall. At first, I was in shock, but as the phone rang again and again, my grief grew angry that friends and family may not be able to attend Emma's memorial service. It is still a mystery to me why thirty-some people, including some immediate family, would be hindered from celebrating Emma's life in person with us because of airport closures.

However, in hindsight, the preliminary event of 9/11 set the stage for a significant memorial on the next day.

Later in the month, one friend wrote the following in a note to us:

"The overwhelming testimony of you and your family in sharing the redemptive nature of her life and death really defied description. The ripples of God's grace may never be fully known by you and yours as a result of that service."

Fortunately, we were privy to some of the churning of God's grace as it poured out through continued conversations and notes. Whether it was as informal as a dinner with friends or as organized as a grief debriefing session with a counselor and twenty-some people, the results were the same. The journey of Emma's life and death took us to new levels of intimacy with relationships old and new. Sitting with one particular friend on his back porch, he described how he witnessed the power of community through her memorial service. That same evening, his wife let us in deeper to her sorrow of losing her two adult-aged brothers. Suffering was slowly and painfully being recycled.

God had to be cheering during these events for He yearns for us to let our politically correct guards down and expose our deepest hurts, fears, insights and emotions. How much more meaningful were those conversations than just the standard ones about our kids, hobbies, the cost of living, and our jobs. Oh, how the mundaneness of life clouds our real stories. But God has a way of using storms to wash away the soot and debris that clouds our lives, causing us to wake up and realize what is really important.

A note from another younger friend, who we've known since she was a freshman in high school, exemplified how a local storm could help wash away her clouded thoughts and grant His perspective. She wrote:

Brian and Missy,

You may have already heard that my husband and I are expecting a baby. It came as an unexpected surprise. For most of the last 16 weeks, I've been going back and forth from the bathroom to bed and wondering how something so small can make me feel so horrible. Without meaning to, I've been becoming increasingly more frustrated and resentful of this unborn child and all the havoc it's been wreaking. You may be wondering what on earth this has to do with anything. So, I'll stop rambling and get to what I really want to share with you.

I never had the privilege of meeting Emma personally until I got to meet her through all the people that shared at her memorial service. I was overwhelmed by how many people she had touched in her short life. Hearing about her love for God and her open willingness to show it really touched my heart. And suddenly, I realized how important children are to the kingdom of God and what an awesome responsibility it is as parents to help them realize that. It's obvious that you both are those kinds of parents.

I got home from the service with a new sense of purpose as a soon-to-be-parent. My prayer is that my child will love God the way that Emma did. I never would've guessed that a two-and-a-half-year-old little girl that I've never met could touch me in a way I've never been touched and filled me with a purpose I could not have otherwise known.

While God recycled our suffering in many ways in the lives of others, one that struck us the most came to our awareness on Emma's first birthday following her death.

Aimee Bailey, my wife's eleven-year-old cousin who lived in Vermont, had spent quite a bit of time with Emma during our visit back in August 2001. She was inspired by her experience with Emma, and wrote a short story about her own realizations:

For my mom and brother, who went through Mother's Day (which fell on Emma's birth date May 12, 2002) and his birthday:

Emma. She will live in my life forever.

The first news of a new cousin brightened my heart. Emma was to arrive in May of 1999. Emma Grace Rhen was thought to be born healthy, only half of her heart functioned properly.

At age two, Emma visited my home. Sadie and Elise, her sisters, had come, too, as well as her parents. Emma seemed to glow from within, showering us with her love and tenderness.

But she was gone all too quickly.

I can still remember her little voice, singing along with the light-up Junior Asparagus toy that she would never let go of. A quiet noise, beautiful, but scratched with asthma. Too soon, the Rhens were off.

I'd never see Emma again.

As my late cousin's birthday comes and goes, my family thinks more and more of Emma, the little butterfly with a broken wing.

She died on September 8th, 2001.

Another unforgettable moment was the phone call my mother received from my grandmother on the day that Emma died.

At first I didn't know who mom was talking to. But soon, her eyes welled up with tears.

"Oh Mutti, I'm so sorry. I'm so sorry!"

With Emma's operations going on this only could mean one thing. And I knew.

"Mom!" I wailed. "How do we tell Livi?" We walked down the steps towards my sister, and said the one sentence that I will never forget:

"Livi, Emma's.............. dead!!!" And we cried together, dreading the moment when my dad and brother came home.

My grandparents flew out for the funeral, which took place on September 12, 2001. The first day of my week long field trip was one of the worst days of my life. Our field trip started on September 11 and I was going to miss the funeral. We didn't know about the attacks on our country, our teachers felt it better not to tell us.

I cried on September 11, but for a different reason than the rest of America did.

And September really hurt me. When I went back to my school, after Camp Pine Knot, there was only one thing that was really hurting me. Emma. But when I came home, it was like stepping into a different world. Though we were in the state of New York for our field trip we had no idea about the tragedy. So all those pictures on the bulletin board at my school didn't make sense to me. But when I got home, I saw the newspaper.

All those lost lives. I knew. I understood. I cried.

My mom tried to comfort me, telling me that her 6th grade year was the hardest too.

But maybe it wasn't my worst year, but my most meaningful. The tragedies of 2001 brought new questions to my mind: What is the meaning of life?

And if life is so short (for some, like Emma, only a fraction of a decade)… who would hate enough to bring death to all those poor people?… To end their lives years ahead of time.

And for what? Nothing, nothing is a good enough reason. No war, not peace.

But maybe people, like terrorists, don't care. Power is all that matters to them. Well, there's more to life than power and government: Love, truth, tenderness, caring. All of these traits Emma had.

And the meaning of life?

Some people, after reading my story, would ask why fragile little Emma was born. I can see why this would be asked. Her poor parents, worrying about her all the time, listening to her little wheezy cough as she ran through the grass, seeing the scar on her chest every time they helped her into her pajamas.

Well my answer is: For two years, Emma's parents were given the joy of having a child, a light from within; to feel the peace and love she radiated off her. I think that Emma helped my family in some way or another.

The thought of her helps me to get over any bridge, whether

an actual bridge, or a bridge of the mind. When I am sick, tired or in pain, I think of Emma, and what she had to go through, at the age of two. Thinking of her, though it sometimes makes me tearful, determines me to continue and forget my pain. Her life had a meaning.

I believe, that Emma, in the two years that she lived, brightened the world of everyone that she knew.

Aimee Bailey
May 12, 2002

When I reflect on Aimee's words all that comes to mind is—how God can recycle even the worst kind of suffering for good.

recycled over and over again

On the one-year anniversary of her death in September 2002, we held a big party at a friend's house to thank everyone who had supported us (we called it Emmaversary). From that time on, our suffering began to be recycled over and over again in a unique seasonal pattern. This pattern would happen every spring and fall over the next five years in a mysterious but comforting consistent rhythm. What began with Bri in March 2002, continued on with others: Tehani, Trevin, Joey, Troy, Gabe, Sydney, and more.

The second round of recycled suffering with Tehani occurred on a beautiful, sunny October Sunday in 2002. I was back to my normal duties overseeing our evening church gathering, after a summer sabbatical that included composing the early part of these lessons learned. During the gathering, after blessing the elements for communion, I headed to the back of our worship center to be available for questions and support of anyone who needed it. There I was, being approached by one of our evening gathering teammates, Donna Misa. She asked if we could talk outside. After we got beyond the exit, she looked me in the eyes and said, "Raye and Tehani are dead!" She then broke into tears.

Raye was the 35-year-old, seven-months-pregnant mother of Tehani, who was almost five. I'd been counseling Raye and her husband, Eddie, Tehani's father, since February. Eddie had survived the minivan accident that ended in the Pacific Ocean after their van plummeted some 200 feet off a cliff just north of Half Moon Bay, CA. When I arrived at Lucile Packard Children's Hospital that night, I found Raye's sister, Robin, and her husband, Gary (Donna's brother), in Tehani's PICU room. Tehani had drowned in the water as the crushed car lay flipped over in the surf. She had been pronounced brain dead, but was on a respirator. The bodies of Raye and the unborn child, Sienna, were at the County Coroner's office. The father, Eddie, who miraculously survived the crash, was in serious condition in the ICU. The situation was surreal and shockingly tragic. Three-fourths of a family was no longer alive, while the surviving father was under suspicion for the accident. In time, he would be convicted and sentenced.

Personally, it was a flashback to our final night with Emma, just over a year prior. Tehani was three rooms down from room 2525 of the PICU, which had been Emma's. On call that night was the familiar face of Dr. Kam, who had released Emma off the respirator and put her into my wife's arms. My favorite nurse, Fred, who had held my mom in his arms, also divinely happened to be on duty. Pastorally, I felt like it was exactly the place I was called to be. Who else on our staff had been down this road? Who else in the county knew this situation or these people so intimately? In addition to counseling Eddie and Raye, I had seen Robin, Gary, and their kids grow in their faith. And sweet Tehani was also a regular with my oldest daughter, Sadie, in their Sunday evening class. Tehani's aunt, Donna, was a faithful single mom who had gotten them all to come to church in the fall of 2001, a few weeks prior to me sharing a message specifically about how God walked us through our life support issues with Emma.

Back then, they could have never envisioned that they would be having to experience a similar life support scene as the one I had described so vividly. As the night unfolded, they had to process similar questions and wrestle with similar issues. Then, they had to face the final decision. My own recall was so vivid as we discussed the key questions and worked through the ethical and theological issues while pondering whether to release her. Then, after deciding to take her off the respirator, I watched the hospital staff initiate the familiar protocol. As the doctors and technicians began to file into Tehani's room, Dr Kam and I followed suit as we walked side by side down the hall. Just prior to entering, he turned to me and asked, "How can you do this? It must be torture to go through this again." I responded, "This is actually soothing to my soul."

After watching Tehani be released from the respirator by the same team that had released Emma a few rooms down the hall only just over a year prior, I stayed with the family until it seemed to be the right time to leave.

As I walked to my car in the moonlit night, I was astonished by the similarity of the events as I reflected on them, yet I was deeply saddened by the difference in the final goodbye. Emma's final moments had a two-year build-up of community, which rose to a crescendo on a final agonizing overcast morning with compassionate friends streaming in to share the grief and say goodbye as she lay in the arms of her mother. There was such beauty in the pain that I have longed to live that day over and over again. However, in a harsh, merciless contrast, Tehani's departure had no build-up or crescendo of a comforting community. It was too sudden, too sterile, too shocking, too shattering, and too isolating for any family to go through. There was no beauty in it—just devastated, crushed souls.

As I drove the short drive home down El Camino Real to Redwood City from the hospital, I could feel the weight of the emotion in my soul rising up. I pulled into a Chevron gas station in Menlo Park, parked near the water and air station, got out of the car, and went in to purchase a bag of Peanut M&Ms and bottled water. When I got back to the car, the flood of emotion came pouring out. My sobbing and breathing were uncontrollable as tears streamed out. I couldn't catch my breath. Looking back, I now know that the layers of anger, gratitude, and deep sadness were being excavated from my soul. It was a painfully rich process that was a necessary part of my personal grief, pastoral release, growth, and calling.

Over the next few years, as the rounds of recycled suffering occurred with other families at that hospital, I found myself often in that same gas station parking spot on the way home after supporting them. The transaction was always the same: Peanut M&Ms, bottled water, sobbing, soul excavation, profound satisfaction, and His presence.

reflection & challenges

In this chapter, what story of recycled suffering impacted you the most and why?

How have seen your suffering recycled?

What about God frustrates or encourages you when it comes to recycled suffering?

EPILOGUE

W ITH OUR THIRD DAUGHTER, Elise, who was six months old at the
time of Emma's death, leaving for her freshman year of college
in September 2019, and our first daughter, Sadie, heading
out to her senior year, my wife and I found ourselves with only our boys,
Noah, fifteen, and Levi, twelve, at home. Though Emma's passing seems
like another lifetime, her photos and the boys' presence in our house are a
regular reminder of the losses and gains from God. The verse on the sign in
the Emma Rhen Memorial Playground, established in 2005, on our church
campus speaks to this loss and gain.

> "The LORD gave and the LORD has taken away; may the
> name of the LORD be praised."

Job 1:21

By having our girls (Sadie, Emma, and Elise) so close together in just over three years, from December 1997 to March 2001, plus Emma leaving so unexpectedly in September 2001, we never thought we'd have more children. Even if Emma had lived, our life would have been full enough with three girls, including one with a heart ailment. However, with her dying, and my wife's sister giving birth to a daughter, Kathryn, who also had a heart condition, it seemed like genetic Russian Roulette for us to have another child. Yet, with Kathryn going on to live a healthy life (to this day), genetic concerns being less than six percent, and some months passing, by January 2002, my faithful and beloved wife, Missy, felt led by God to have another child. Personally, I was terrified, but willing. After a year of infertility in 2002, Noah (November 2003) was gifted to us by God, and Levi (March 2007) followed just over three years later.

Looking back, it seems odd how such loss and gain could be so close together. The despair of watching Missy hold Emma as she faded into eternity on that gray morning of September 8, 2001, contrasted with such joy as I watched Noah squirm as he was placed on my wife's chest, post birth, on the bright morning of November 12, 2003. Those events seemed like they should be a lifetime apart, not just barely two years.

What I realize now is that the counterbalance of our loss and gain in children, along with the endless movements of recycled suffering over the years, made Emma's departure so much more bearable and acceptable. Like Job, who lost it all, but gained back double in the second half of his life, so has been our experience. I have pastored enough over the last twenty-five years to know that this counterbalance does not always take place. The grief scale for so many remains weighted to the side of loss, with no counterbalance of gain in sight. Because this ends up being so painfully unfair, I felt the need to publish these lessons learned so others could understand, manage, and survive grief of every kind.

Webster's Dictionary and others may define grief differently, yet I have come to define grief in the following manner:

> A complex emotional state that comes when one has a loss of expectations hoped for.

People all around us are grieving on a daily basis and we are unaware. The loss of expectations hoped for culminates in a grief fog enveloping them that we cannot see. Some are grieving the past, present, and future. Some are grieving what they did not receive as a child from a father or mother, the cruel treatment or betrayal of a spouse, the death of a loved one, the loss of a job, the inability to get pregnant, and the list goes on and on. Young and old grieve throughout all life stages. The only thing that is capable of satisfying one's grief is a perspective from God, and that is what I believe these lessons represent.

Hence, my hope is that these lessons will help to counterbalance your despair of grief. So may you receive them, ponder them, let them be salve to your grieving soul, and then graciously pass on what you have learned to comfort another.

To go to heaven, fully to enjoy God,
is infinitely better than the most
pleasant accommodations here.

Jonathan Edwards

AFTERWORD

life in heaven

I N THE EARLY DAYS AFTER LOSING EMMA, the only thing I yearned for was to be in heaven. Life seemed mundane and meaningless after such an ordeal. Though I was not suicidal, I did not care to live without my daughter. The grief would culminate each week in our Sunday evening church gathering, which I continued to pastor. During worship singing time, I intentionally positioned myself in the front row, which gave me the best view out the floor-to-ceiling windows, nearly four stories high. In this particular spot, I would peer into the endless sky in the presence of God, while surrounded by music that captured my soul. Crying out my pain as I sang to the beyond, I yearned for my little Emma and wondered what heaven was like.

heaven is better

Until then, I had never cared much about heaven. Being raised in an Irish Catholic home in southwestern Pennsylvania that was religious in Sunday mass and holy day rituals, but not integrated in relationship with God during the week, my early belief in God and heaven was on a low simmer of intrigue without engagement by the time I left for college. However, by 1991, with Missy's influence as my college girlfriend, and a few other Christians I had met since moving to California, my realization that I didn't understand and hadn't experienced God became very apparent. Specifically, they helped me understand that it was not just about believing in God, but also about making a genuine commitment to following Him. The gift of my consistent Catholic upbringing was that it had solidified my belief in God. But I had no idea what it meant to follow Him. To add to that, by my early twenties, I lacked peace and self-worth, for I was haunted by shame and guilt based on my imperfections and past destructive behavior. Meanwhile, I was questioning the purpose of life as I began my first job. Based on the combination of my faith background and present circumstances, I was ripe for an awakening.

That awakening turned out to be me realizing how much God loved me, gifted me, and wanted me to be His child, regardless of my striving and sinfulness. Comprehending the crucifixion and resurrection of Jesus released me from my shame and guilt, resulting in long-lasting freedom. Discovering how the Holy Spirit was willing to partner with me to follow God in a new kingdom way, one that reflected His love and character, empowered me with purpose like I'd never had before. Even with this awakening, getting into heaven still wasn't a motivation for me. The concept of a heavenly eternity with God was only icing on this new-found cake of realization.

In time, even as a pastor, I never used heaven to entice people into a relationship with God. I had felt that heaven was much too distant for our impulsive culture. I disliked how heaven was also often used as a carrot or even a scare tactic to begin a relationship with Him. I felt as though peace on earth, unconditional love from God, and His purpose for our lives was enough to draw in our overloaded, love-starved, easily distracted culture. However, Emma's relocation from earth, coupled with intense conversations with friends and colleagues about heaven, sparked my desire to know more about the truth of this eternal place.

The challenge of trying to understand heaven is obvious. No one who has been there has come back to tell us first-hand what it was like, except Jesus. Consequently, we are dependent on history books, theories of world religions, and mysterious stories from those who claim to have been there for a moment or more and then come back. For this reason alone, I cannot wait to die and get there. As long as I am alive, I will attempt to live life to the fullest, yet my limited life so far on earth tells me that heaven must be better. After experiencing fifty-plus years of life, which has included school, several jobs, accepting God's love, marrying the woman I fell deeply in love with, finding my calling, raising five unique children, losing a little one I loved, having just enough money, then having more money than we needed, tasting all the food I ever wanted, traveling to other countries, officiating weddings and memorials, carrying other's burdens, seeing my parents decline, and observing the pain and destruction in this world, I believe and hope there is a place even more satisfying.

The views on the afterlife are different depending on what world religion or faith community you choose. So when you get into a discussion of heaven, you have to ask the questions: Are we all talking about the same heaven, but from different perspectives? Is it like the men who are surrounding a massive elephant? One is holding onto and describing the tail, while the other describes the ear. They each have a different perspective, but it is the same elephant they are talking about. This begs the question: Is there only one absolute truth about heaven? Sean McDowell, professor, author, and speaker wrote in an article the following:

"According to a Barna Study, 58% of teens and 62% of adults agree with the statement, 'Many religions can lead to eternal life (heaven); there is no one true religion.'

It would be nice if everybody could be right about their religious convictions. After all, these are beliefs we often hold dear to our hearts. Nobody likes telling others that they are wrong about their deepest convictions. Yet simple reason and common sense tell us all religions cannot possibly be true.

By its very nature, truth is exclusive. It is not logically possible for all religions to be right when their core claims differ so radically. Either they are all wrong, or one is right."[11]

Of all world religions, Jesus was the only leader to claim he was God.

"I and the Father are one."

John 10:30

The rest could only claim to be messengers of God, mere prophets. Furthermore, of these prophets who claimed status with Jesus, only He was conceived of a virgin, sinless in His actions, performed miracles, and was resurrected from the dead. Plus, Jesus is the only one to claim that access to heaven comes by way of His grace and our faith in it—not by works.

The words of Jesus help us to understand that there is a physical place that we will go to:

"Do not let your hearts be troubled. You believe in God; believe also in me. My Father's house has many rooms; if that were not so, would I have told you that I am going there to prepare a place for you? And if I go and prepare a place for you, I will come back and take you to be with me that you also may be where I am."

John 14:1-3

Am I convinced it is an actual house as we understand houses? No. We are limited in our ability to grasp the specifics of heaven, and Jesus was attempting to share an analogy that would bring comfort and understanding.

What's often misunderstood is that there are several heavenly realms. The first of the current heavenly realms is the physical earth, including the stars and skies. In the Bible, God continually taught man using this first heaven with references to stars, wind, birds and grass. We can see, experience, and learn how God is a provider and sustainer from this realm, but we are not called to worship the creation. The second heaven is the unseen spiritual realm surrounding the earth where angels and Satan exist. It is not physical in nature and unidentifiable to most. The third heaven, the one we most often think of and refer to, is where God, Jesus, and believers who have already passed away currently dwell. The Bible actually uses the term "third heaven" in 2 Corinthians 12:2. It is referring to the third heaven that all who believe in Jesus will ultimately enter.

The current heavens are different from the new heaven that will come when Jesus returns to earth. In this futuristic event, only grasped by using our sci-fi mentality, the third heaven will come to earth. In essence, the portion of the Lord's Prayer "on earth as it is in heaven" from Matthew 6:10 will manifest itself before our very eyes. All three heavens and earth will become one. There, believer bodies will be resurrected fully from the earth and dwell with God, Jesus, the angels, and other believers on this newly combined heaven and earth. However, prior to the coming of Christ, when one dies, only their spirit is with God in the third heaven, while their body or ashes wait to be resurrected into a full body upon Jesus's return and the development of the new heaven and earth. Consequently, I believe that Emma's spirit is with God today. When Jesus returns and the heavens and earth combine, the bodies of all believers who have passed away, including hers and mine, will be resurrected and spend eternity together.

At what age or stage of life will her body be? I am not sure. This is part of the reason I am eager to go. The apostle John gives us a glimpse of the development of the new heaven and earth:

> "Then I saw 'a new heaven and a new earth,' for the first heaven and the first earth had passed away, and there was no longer any sea. I saw the Holy City, the new Jerusalem, coming down out of heaven from God, prepared as a bride beautifully dressed for her husband. And I heard a loud voice from the throne saying, 'Look! God's dwelling place is now among the people, and he will dwell with them. They will be his people, and God himself will be with them and be their God. He will wipe every tear from their eyes. There will be no more death or mourning or crying or pain, for the old order of things has passed away."
>
> **Revelation 21:1-4**

The apostle Paul gives us an extensive perspective on what will happen to our bodies in the new heaven:

> "But someone may ask, 'How will the dead be raised? What kind of bodies will they have?' What a foolish question! When you put a seed into the ground, it doesn't grow into a plant unless it dies first. And what you put in the ground is not the plant that will grow, but only a bare seed of wheat or whatever you are planting. Then God gives it the new body he wants it to have. A different plant grows from each kind of seed. Similarly there are different kinds of flesh—one kind for

humans, another for animals, another for birds, and another for fish. There are also bodies in the heavens and bodies on the earth. The glory of the heavenly bodies is different from the glory of the earthly bodies. The sun has one kind of glory, while the moon and stars each have another kind. And even the stars differ from each other in their glory."

1 Corinthians 15:35-41 (NLT)

These passages guarantee us how gloriously unique heaven will be. Death will bring new life. It will be different than on earth. It's human nature to struggle with the unknown, but our loving God knows what's best for us. In the same passage, Paul goes on into greater details about our specific bodies:

"It is the same way with the resurrection of the dead. Our earthly bodies are planted in the ground when we die, but they will be raised to live forever. Our bodies are buried in brokenness, but they will be raised in glory. They are buried in weakness, but they will be raised in strength... We will not all die, but we will all be transformed! It will happen in a moment, in the blink of an eye, when the last trumpet is blown. For when the trumpet sounds, those who have died will be raised to live forever. And we who are living will also be transformed. For our dying bodies must be transformed into bodies that will never die..."

1 Corinthians 15:42-43, 51-53 (NLT)

These passages guarantee our bodies to be Christ-like. We will be holy and pure in nature, filled with power forever. In the new heaven and earth, our current earthly mission of continually allowing the Holy Spirit to transform us into the likeness of Christ (2 Cor. 3:18) will be accomplished. Finally, Paul goes on to tell us what we will be doing in this new heaven once the heavenly trumpet sounds.

> "Then, when our dying bodies have been transformed into bodies that will never die, this Scripture will be fulfilled: 'Death is swallowed up in victory. O death, where is your victory? O death, where is your sting?'"

1 Corinthians 15: 54-55 (NLT)

This concluding passage guarantees a victory party. The painful sting of death will no longer pierce us. We will celebrate by praising God. John tells us how this will look:

> "Then I looked and heard the voice of many angels, numbering thousands upon thousands, and ten thousand times ten thousand. They encircled the throne and the living creatures and the elders. In a loud voice they were saying: 'Worthy is the Lamb, who was slain, to receive power and wealth and wisdom and strength and honor and glory and praise!' Then I heard every creature in heaven and on earth and under the earth and on the sea, and all that is in them, saying: 'To him who sits on the throne and to the Lamb be praise and honor and glory and power, FOR EVER AND EVER!' The four living creatures said, 'Amen,' and the elders fell down and worshiped."

Revelation 5:11-14

How wonderful it will be to share in that celebration with Emma someday!

reflection & challenges

Is heaven motivating for you? Why or why not?

What has impacted your view of heaven the most?

How do the Scriptures from this chapter reshape your view of heaven?

EMMA'S PARK
DEDICATION

FAITHFUL DONATIONS FROM FRIENDS, FAMILY, and the attendees of the Greater Latrobe Basketball Golf Outing (2003) provided for the opening of the Emma Rhen Memorial Park on the Peninsula Covenant Church campus. This dream was envisioned by Missy for preschool children and their parents to enjoy.

At the dedication on April 24, 2005, a large group of us sang, cried, and gave thanks to God while having these words and Scripture read:

A Reflection: Ashes to Glory

Her illness humbled us as we lost control.

Her life of two years forced us to include Him and others more.

Her death brought perspective and depth to life.

The sting of loss has been replaced by the sweetness of thoughts.

The question of "why?" has been displaced by the experiences of suffering recycled for good.

His Word, prayer, community and reflection have been the methods of His power and grace.

God, the Father, has allowed it and provided for us.

Christ exemplified how a death can bring a more abundant life.

The Spirit has been salve to our wounds of grief.

Like Job in the latter part of life, we stand restored by Him, blessed beyond our imagination and in awe.

Though provided by an extended community of friends and family, we acknowledge this park as God's, for only He could take a foundation of ash and use it for such glory.

"…so after you have suffered a little while, he will restore, support, and strengthen you, and he will place you on a firm foundation."

1 Peter 5:10 (NLT)

NOTES

1 Frederick Buechner, *Wishful Thinking: A Theological ABC*, (New York: HarperOne, 1993).

2 C.S. Lewis, *A Grief Observed*, (New York: HarperCollins, 2001).

3 *The Daily Walk Bible (NIV)*, (Carol Stream, IL: Tyndale House, 1997).

4 *The Daily Walk Bible (NIV)*.

5 *The Daily Walk Bible (NIV)*.

6 Ruth Haley Barton, *Sacred Rhythms: Arranging Our Lives for Spiritual Transformation*, (Downers Grove, IL: IVP Intervarsity Press, 2006).

7 Dallas Willard, *The Allure of Gentleness: Defending the Faith in the Manner of Jesus*, (New York: HarperOne, 2015).

8 Wayne Grudem, *Systematic Theology*, (Grand Rapids, MI: Zondervan, 1994).

9 Henri J. M. Nouwen, *The Wounded Healer*, (New York: Doubleday, 1979).

10 Nouwen, *The Wounded Healer*.

11 Sean McDowell, "Can All Religions Be True? No Way!" *SeanMcDowell.org* (blog), January 17, 2019, https://seanmcdowell.org/blog/can-all-religions-be-true-no-way.

ABOUT
BRIAN H. RHEN

For over twenty-five years, Brian has been guiding people along the best pathway for their life with God.

Shaped by a Western Pennsylvania Irish Catholic upbringing, a recovery background, a Protestant spiritual renewal, an imperfect marriage of almost three decades, the death of one of his five children, a pastoral career, much failure and some success, his style is authentic and practical.

Schooled in a Bachelors of Science (Management) from Bucknell University and a Master of Divinity (Pastoral Care) from Western Seminary, his use of psychology, neuroscience, coaching, and spiritual direction highly influences his approach and practice. His mode of guidance is done best one-to-one, one-to-two, or in groups large and small.

Since 1995, he and his wife have been raising and launching their five children into this world and heaven as he has served at Peninsula Covenant Church in Redwood City, California.

For contact, resources or services go to brianrhen.com.

MALAWI
CHILDREN'S
MISSION

10% of all proceeds from this book will go to Malawi Children's Mission (MCM), which was formed in 2007 to serve orphaned and vulnerable children in the Lirangwe area, north of the city of Blantyre in Malawi, Africa.

For more information:
malawichildrensmission.org